Awakening
YOUR PATH

Awakening
YOUR PATH

Christy Godwin & Iris Libby

WingStar
Publishing

First edition, published in the United States by WingStar Publishing, 2025.

ISBN Hardcover: 979-8-9986762-1-5
ISBN Paperback: 979-8-9986762-0-8
ISBN Audiobook: 979-8-9986762-2-2
ISBN Electronic: 979-8-9986762-3-9

Library of Congress Control Number: 2025908687

Author's Note: WingStar Publishing and this book's authors provide this book and any related accompanying materials for informational purposes only. Anything stated in this book should NOT be taken as a replacement for medical, clinical, or professional advice, diagnosis, or medical intervention. If you take any action based on the contents of this book, this is based solely on your decision, and the publisher and authors cannot be held liable for any of the consequences of such action or inaction.

Acknowledgments

To our incredible team—Jason, Margot, and Nicolette—
Your brilliance, dedication, and creative vision breathed life into this book. Your expert guidance, thoughtful edits, and genuine care helped shape every chapter into something meaningful. Awakening Your Path would not be what it is without your unique contributions. We are endlessly grateful.

To Christy's family, and especially to her husband Ken—
Thank you for your patience, your love, and for enduring many long days and nights while Christy disappeared into the world of words. This book wouldn't exist without your quiet strength.

To Iris's friends who have become her family—
Your love, support, and unwavering presence have been a guiding light. You've held space through the highs and the lows, and your belief in this work—and in Iris—has meant the world. Thank you for being home in human form.

To our dear friends who helped us hone The Process—
Thank you for being willing participants in the early stages of The Process. Your openness, honesty, and thoughtful feedback helped us fine-tune what worked, and more importantly, what didn't. Your courage to explore with us, to speak truthfully, and to trust the unfolding journey made all the difference. This work is better, deeper, and more aligned because of you.

To everyone who has ever triggered us—
You've been our unexpected teachers. Through discomfort and challenge, you helped us grow, reflect, and rise. Thank you for unknowingly holding the mirror that led us back to ourselves.

With deep gratitude,

Christy & Iris

Contents

Foreword ix

Preface xi

The Door 1

Triggers 13

The Lens Through Which We View the World 31

Awareness & Self-Reflection 53

Change Versus Transformation 73

Faith in the Unseen World 89

Pure Soul & True Essence 106

Self-Love, Boundaries & Neutrality 123

The Process 141

Case Studies 145

Worksheet 165

Epilogue 171

About the Authors 173

Foreword

By Richard Martini, author of Hacking the Afterlife

Some people enter your life for a season. Others walk in and never leave—because they had somehow always been with you. That's how I feel about Iris Libby. We met way back in high school, and somehow, the connection always felt like it predated lockers and lunch bells. When someone you connect with feels like a soul you've always known, you pay attention.

So when Iris told me she and Christy Godwin were writing a book together, my ears perked up. I already knew Iris had one foot on this side of the great cosmic classroom and one foot on the other side—we've worked together for years on the kinds of sessions and soul journeys that most people only whisper about. I've seen her channel mind-blowing wisdom from beyond the veil, and I've watched her sit with people—clients, friends, strangers—and reflect back the truth of who they really are.

Iris is a gifted astrologer, psychic medium, and trance channeler with decades of experience helping people find their paths. But what makes her unique is how she blends all of that spiritual insight with sharp business acumen. She has led major organizations at the highest levels, making decisions under immense pressure—while quietly using her intuition to guide the whole operation. From the boardroom to the spirit realm, she's lived both lives with integrity and clarity. And she brings all of that into this book: the vision, the practicality, and the wisdom earned through real transformation.

Then there's Christy Godwin—a powerhouse of her own. An exceptional medium, healer, and life coach, Christy works with extraordinary clarity and compassion. She connects people with departed loved ones, clears deep emotional and energetic obstacles, and empowers people to reclaim their lives with fierce grace. Whether she's channeling a message, guiding a client through trauma, or helping someone unlock their inner strength, Christy leads with heart and unshakable knowing.

Her background is equally impressive. She's taught for over 30 years, holds degrees in child development and finance, and is certified in nearly every major healing modality you can name—Akashic Records, Reiki, hypnotherapy, you name it. But above all that, what strikes you most about Christy is her deep devotion to helping others live freely, fully, and with purpose.

What Christy and Iris have created together in Awakening Your Path is more than a book—it's a spiritual toolkit. This book is for anyone who's ever asked "Why do I react like this?" or "Why can't I move forward?" or "What's really holding me back?" Through personal insight, deep wisdom, and decades of experience, Iris and Christy walk you through how to identify and release the emotional triggers that keep us stuck. These aren't just vague concepts—they're patterns, programs, and pain points that many of us carry without realizing it. And this book shows you how to let them go.

What makes this book so powerful is that it doesn't just talk about transformation, it guides you through it. These two don't hide behind abstract spiritual language or lofty ideas. They offer step-by-step support, real tools, and hard-won wisdom from their own paths. You're not reading theory here. You're walking alongside two people who have done the deep work and are brave enough to share the map.

If you've been spinning your wheels in therapy, repeating old patterns, or feeling like something's missing no matter how many books you read— take heart. Awakening Your Path is the star that will steer you back to your true life's journey of fulfillment. This is the book that sits you down, looks you in the eye, and says, "Let's go deeper. Let's clear it out. Let's get free." That's why I'm telling you to read it—not because I love these women, but because I've seen what they can do. And if you let it guide you through the work of self-reflection this book can be life changing.

So yes, I'm biased. I love these two. But I also know greatness when I see it. Read this book, take it seriously, and let it open the door to a new kind of freedom. Because that's what Iris and Christy do best—they help people come home to themselves. Welcome Home.

Preface

Hello, beautiful souls! It is no accident that you are holding this book in your hands. Something within you—perhaps a quiet whisper or a deep knowing—has guided you here. *Awakening Your Path* was born from a calling to help those on their spiritual journey navigate life with greater clarity, wisdom, and love.

In these pages, you will find a process—one that we have fine-tuned through years of experience, personal transformation, and guiding others through their own awakenings. This is not a rigid set of rules but rather a compassionate approach to self-discovery, healing, and empowerment. We believe true growth comes from honoring your own path, learning to trust yourself, and embracing both the light and the shadows within.

The Process we share is designed to help you release old patterns, heal deep wounds, and reconnect with the powerful, intuitive being that you already are. It is a journey of remembering—remembering your worth, your strength, and the love that has always been within you.

As you move through this book, we invite you to give yourself grace. Healing is not linear, and transformation does not happen overnight. But with patience, persistence, and a willingness to show up for yourself, you will find that you are capable of more than you ever imagined.

Thank you for allowing us to walk alongside you on this journey. May you move forward with an open heart, trusting that every step—no matter how small—is leading you home to yourself.

With much love and light,

Christy & Iris

Chapter 1

The Door

You are now standing at the doorway to your path, and we—Christy and Iris—welcome you! By making the decision to open this book to the first page, you have taken your first step towards what can be an energizing, exciting, and to be honest, tumultuous journey towards self-discovery. We have poured our lives and love onto the pages of this book with the intention of offering you The Process, a tool you can use regardless of where you are right now in your life. Our hope is that you use The Process to dig deep into yourself—your past and present experiences, fulfilled, and unfulfilled desires—to uncover your authentic self, and as you do this, to discover your capacity to live and love every day, joyfully and with a peaceful heart. Whether you are struggling now or simply wish to open yourself more fully to your innate wisdom, we are here as your guides as you awaken your soul's path.

As we are asking you to trust us to help you find your own truth and your own path, let us begin by telling you more about who we are and how we found ourselves this path.

Meet Christy

You have more control than you think.

If my years as a medium and psychic have taught me anything, it is this. The deepest pain you feel, the kind you believe is too ingrained to ever be removed, can be eased and managed. We are all in constant communication with the realm of spirit, whether we know it or not. While I have been receiving messages from spirits since childhood, it is in the last decade when I've honed these abilities and, alongside astrologer and fellow spiritual advisor Iris Libby, used them to spread healing, enlightenment, and easement from pain to as many people as possible.

Awakening Your Path is more than just a book. This path is an entire journey, one beginning with a locked door on an ordinary day. Behind this mundane obstacle was the start of something extraordinary: the birth of the enlightenment method which we fondly call The Process.

The purpose of The Process is not to teach mediumship or spirituality. This is a process of healing, available to anyone and everyone. The truth is, we all possess some degree of psychic ability, and the realm of spirit interacts with us every moment of every day, regardless of whether we are consciously aware. The Process is here to teach you how to harness the energy you are already in contact with and direct it within yourself in search of healing and love. How often do you look within and discover something you experienced years earlier has been informing your actions? Do you find yourself behaving in a way you know is out of line with who you are deep inside? Feeling like we cannot control our own emotions and deeds can be some of the most isolating and desperate moments of our lives.

In those moments, who is in control?

Often, the answer is the past. We all have had experiences that harmed us, and no one can experience trauma without it somehow informing who we become afterward. When our pain is triggered, even by something small, it can send us down a spiral of turmoil, self-doubt, and negative intrusive thoughts. We may feel unable to stop the stream of these thoughts that seem to come from nowhere; however, we can learn to recognize that these thoughts are simply thoughts that can be managed and put to rest.

We have come to call this type of reaction to an experience that causes pain as a "trigger." While this word can mean different things to different people, in general it can be thought of as something that causes a strong emotional reaction for a person. Often that reaction seems to come from nowhere and can appear to be blown out of proportion.

Though it may feel as though we are powerless against our thought patterns, it's essential to remember that these patterns are simply habits— ingrained ways of thinking we've developed over time. And like any habit, with effort, patience, and a deep compassion for ourselves, these thought patterns can be changed. We are not prisoners of our minds; we have the capacity to reshape our mental landscapes, even when this seems daunting.

The word "trigger" has become a buzzword in our culture today, used in many different contexts. We will explore this concept more fully later, but I bring it up here because you might be reading this and thinking, "You don't understand. My emotional triggers run too deep; they'll never let me live the life I want." If that resonates with you, I want you to know that there is hope.

Triggers often stem from deep emotional wounds, and while they may feel overwhelming, they are not insurmountable. The process of healing is not about erasing or ignoring those triggers; it's about learning to navigate through them with love, understanding, and compassion for yourself. By gently working with your mind rather than against it, you can begin to shift your emotional responses and break free from patterns that may have held you back for years.

With consistent diligence, self-love, and self-compassion, you can start to unravel these patterns. Change doesn't happen overnight, and it may require more patience than you initially expect, but the ability to awaken your path is worth it. The process of healing and self-growth can open doors to a life you've only dreamed of living before—a life rooted in peace, clarity, and self-love.

Even if you feel this does not apply to you and you have learned to manage your triggers well, I invite you to continue reading. We all carry emotional burdens and scars which can be triggered without our conscious awareness. If you are someone who has developed the skill to conceal emotional outbursts or suppress inappropriate reactions, it does not necessarily mean you have effectively dealt with and processed your triggers in a way which promotes emotional well-being.

As you walk on your path of release, you will gradually unveil layers, revealing deeper triggers. As each successive layer dissipates, you experience a heightened sense of lightness, serenity, and an enhanced capacity to navigate your life journey with renewed confidence and a profound sense of joy. You begin to feel empowered, knowing you have the ability to face any circumstance coming your way.

At this point, The Process might sound intimidating or even invasive. But The Process is a tool: a series of questions devised to reveal, investigate, and eventually eliminate these triggers. It does not require equipment, resources, or even outside assistance, once you've learned how to use it. The Process comes from you. The dedication it requires, as well as the healing it brings, is yours and yours alone, originating and developing within you. It uses your own energy and faith to ease your pain and, yes, awaken your path.

It is crucial to acknowledge that your readiness is paramount in awakening your path and releasing triggers. Without this readiness, even if you earnestly engage in the steps to address the trigger, achieving complete release may remain elusive. However, even in a state of unreadiness, The Process serves as a valuable tool by fostering heightened awareness of the underlying issue. Indeed, the more awareness we bring to such issues, the greater the potential for improvement and healing.

When people come to me, as a psychic medium, they often already know the answers to their questions; my role is to help them realize their feelings and intuitions are an internal guidance system with a direct link to their soul's desires. I assist them in opening up their own gifts to navigate their lives, while simultaneously encouraging them to tap into spirit themselves. I feel truly blessed to have walked alongside thousands of individuals, supporting them as they awaken to their unique paths—

paths that lead to a fuller, lighter, and more enlightened way of being. If you've found yourself reading this book, trust that you are meant to be here, guided by your own inner wisdom.

You may hold the idea common in pop culture—psychic mediumship is somehow unnatural or constructed, or only a select few possess these abilities from birth. These false beliefs only serve to cut us off from a love greater than ourselves and the guidance readily available to us. By reclaiming this natural skill, we can reconnect with the profound support and wisdom the spiritual realm offers.

This is a lesson I had to learn myself. Born and raised in Louisiana, now living in Omaha, I had already checked the classic boxes of society— getting an education, marrying my husband of thirty-eight years, having children, and involving myself in my community. Although I was content with my life, I sensed there was more I had yet to achieve. As my children grew older, they, along with my husband, often joked about my knack for predicting things. Once, my husband asked me, "Do you ever get tired of always being right?"

Of course, I replied, "No, not really!"

I had not always realized the importance of my past mystical experiences, since communication with spirits does not resemble everyday verbal conversation. The profound contact with spirits and the shifts in energy which led me to predict events months or years before they happened eventually convinced me to hone the gift I had been given. I had taken several mediumship courses before enrolling in a course where I met Iris. I had been pulled there for some reason, and the reason is now clear.

Since our work together began, Iris and I frequently bring through messages for each other—it was through these joint messages from spirit we learned we were meant to work together. We did not decide to seek out this path. When professional psychic mediums are together, we do what comes naturally, bringing up spirits, tapping into situations psychically, and channeling. Awakening Your Path and the development of The Process was born from one of these sessions. Iris and I just followed the energetic path leading to this simple yet brilliant process.

Iris refers to me as the "spirit machine," since I am in constant contact with the spirit realm, holding complete conversations with passed loved ones, guides, and other entities. I should mention, though, I feel the same way about her: Iris is the most phenomenal channeler I have ever witnessed. Her connection is instantaneous and pure, never letting ego interfere or cloud her messages.

The messages we began receiving gave me pause as to what I would be doing and the potential healing impact I would have on others. Though some of the same information had been coming to me in meditations, I felt inadequate for the task at hand.

Becoming closer to the divine vibration of God has always been of utmost importance, and I know how it feels to fail in moments when I have not lived up to the commitment. The information in my meditations matched exactly with what spirit was telling Iris, as well as several other mediums who approached me about my purpose. Whether I liked it or not, I realized my life was about to change, and I was going to forge a pivotal path.

Iris and I could not be more different on the surface. But while we differ in demographics and personality, we are completely in sync spiritually. As soon as the beginnings of The Process revealed themselves to us, we began working on it with gusto and passion. The questions have gone through many varying stages before crystallizing into the finished Process you will experience through this book. They have been tested and reworked using friends, peers, and strangers, who each in their own way have contributed to the voyage we invite you to embark upon. Close colleagues and dubious skeptics alike have gone through The Process and come out with their triggers eased.

My training in hypnotherapy, neuro-linguistic programming (NLP), and many other modalities played a significant role in shaping the questions. While this can make the work sound complicated or inaccessible, what makes The Process truly remarkable is its simplicity. Throughout its development, we constantly kept simplicity in mind, striving to maintain it even as we considered adding more elements. The importance of simplicity cannot be overstated.

After developing the original set of questions, Iris and I took them and enthusiastically began the refinement stage through collaborative workshops. We actively sought input from our friends, gauging the effectiveness of the questions as we used them to guide friends through their own challenges. Sometimes when you're deeply entrenched in a particular field, it is easy to overlook what others may not be aware of. Our collaborative efforts shed light on the need for educational support if we wanted participants to fully grasp the benefits of The Process.

Our initial encounter, which took place online, could be described as pleasantly unremarkable. What lingers vividly in my memory is the impression Iris left on me—a person of undeniable talent, exuding immense energy, further accentuated by her distinctive red lipstick, which I still love to this day.

It was not until time had gracefully unfolded itself that the profound implications of our meeting revealed themselves. It is a reminder that some of life's most meaningful connections often come in quiet moments, carrying the potential to blossom into transformative journeys. Looking back, I am in awe of how fate intervened, as she always does.

So... how could one locked door lead to all this? And how can you benefit from the discoveries you have yet to make? Let Iris and I be your guides on this beautiful expedition of living the awakened and more joyful life you have been searching for. The two of us were brought together by forces larger than ourselves, forces determined to help us create The Process outlined in this book.

Meet Iris

I had been circling the hotel for forty-five minutes when I decided to disregard the smoke. There wasn't a sign in sight. In fact, besides the row of doors facing the parking lot, there was no indication this was a hotel at all, and the only people I could ask for help were a couple who stood under the flickering lights of the awning, smoking a mysterious substance out of a narrow glass pipe. Huh, I thought, "What am I doing here?"

Pushing aside my doubts, I went inside to meet my fellow classmates. I had spent the last nine months in an online course, which would end here, this week, with group testing and eventual certification as a Spiritual Advisor. This would be my first time meeting my classmates in person, and I had absolutely no idea what to expect from them. As we mingled and made introductions, one classmate, Christy Godwin, touched my arm, and bam! At that moment, I felt my path shift again.

Most of us may not realize how often a single moment changes our lives. It could be as straightforward as turning the right corner at the right moment or putting the perfect shirt on one morning. One of the benefits of tapping into our psychic intuition is a clearer view of the unknown, and if we listen well, we can feel when one choice—or, in this case, one meeting—is going to change everything.

From my early childhood, I had known things I had no reason to know. I had always tried to ignore it, and as I got older, I waved it off as good instincts and plenty of luck. Rising through the ranks of the business world, I was always the oddball mystic in a room full of skeptics. I began to study astrology in my free time, offering readings to close friends and referrals.

In 2020, while the world was flipping upside down, my astrological chart practically screamed at me to follow suit. So, I decided to sell my executive recruitment firm and dive headfirst into making astrology my full-time job.

In October 2020, I was deep into a private astrology reading for a client who claimed their sleep was haunted by ghostly hangouts with dearly departed friends and family. I suggested he take some classes to manage these spectral visits. But as I was researching classes for him, an unexpected voice piped up in my head, insisting I sign myself up for a nine-month course on mediumship and psychic abilities. Talk about the universe sending a not-so-subtle nudge!

I brushed it off, but it just wouldn't shut up for the rest of the evening and well into the night. But I'm an astrologer, I reasoned, without much use for certification as a medium or psychic. The voice was adamant. Finally, I gave in, and by 11:57 PM, I was enrolled in Lisa Williams's online Spiritual Advisor™ Certification course. The next day, I discovered that the registration deadline had been midnight. Clearly, the more I ignored the spirit's nagging voice, the louder the message got. Lesson learned: spirits don't do subtle.

So after nine long months of online instruction, here I was, standing in the dodgy hotel with Christy Godwin's hand on my arm. The only opinion I had of Christy at this point was immense respect for her talent. Over Zoom, I had witnessed her summon eight spirits in under half an hour without dropping her composure for a second. Now, meeting her in person, my casual respect for this bona fide spirit machine turned into astonishment. An image appeared to me, as sharp as the words on this page. As our skin connected, I saw Christy and me working together on a stage, discussing spirituality and religion before an audience. This vision revealed an unbreakable connection between us, put in place by the universe itself.

We spent the week engaging in testing exercises, including meditation and cold readings. Through these, Christy and I quickly discovered that we could communicate nonverbally. During one group meditation, my back was killing me, something that's all too common. I hadn't mentioned it to the group. But during the session, I felt Christy's energy reach out to me, flitting up and down my back like a butterfly. In a room full of people, there was no mistake who had done it. The pain subsided. When the meditation was over, we locked eyes, and I thanked her. She had never healed someone without their express permission, she explained. But she had asked permission, and I had given it. No words required.

The connection we shared once we began talking was just as startling. On paper, Christy and I had, and still have, almost nothing in common. She, an Omaha military wife and mother, who truly walks in the love of Christianity. Her Louisiana upbringing makes her as polite as she is no-nonsense. Me, a Jewish, radical lesbian New Yorker with beyond-left politics and a penchant to shoot from the hip. With me, what you see is what you get. These material differences are what make our partnership such a powerful one. I push where she holds back, she reflects as I forge ahead. She brings out in me my highest moral values and makes me want to commit to the highest good for everyone. I never let her forget what she's here for, where her talents lie, and how to trust herself enough to share them. At the end of the day, any difference in our backgrounds is meaningless. We saw each other, on this plane and beyond, and we knew that together, we were a powerhouse team with a job to do.

The two of us were attached at the hip for the rest of the week. When it was over, our exams finished, and our certifications complete, it seemed bizarre to say goodbye to Christy. After we had parted, we spoke constantly over the phone and on video calls. We began to meditate together in the mornings. We planned excursions, and I traveled to her home in Nebraska, while she traveled to my (polar opposite) home in Southern California. Physically, we were living in different worlds, but our higher connection transcended it all.

Through this time, we began to brainstorm ideas for our project together, keeping in mind my vision of us together on stage. It was clear our connection was both powerful and truly vital to both of us, and the decision to work together had already been made. We knew the right path was going to not only reveal itself but announce itself with big old horns and fireworks. And it did.

During one of Christy's visits at my home, we embarked on a five-hour silent meditation. Before we had even begun, I found myself with doubts. Silence is really, really not my thing. How could I sit in a room with anyone else for that long and not say a word?

I lasted an hour before I began to squirm. I tried as hard as I could to contain myself, but after ninety minutes of complete silence, I broke.

"How can you do this?" I blurted.

Christy looked at me matter-of-factly and said, "I could be silent for the rest of my life."

This response astounded me. I stood and left Christy to her peace. For the next several hours, I was bouncing off the walls, in search of something to do. I needed a playmate! I wondered again how I could ever have agreed to a silent meditation, when one of my most cherished pastimes has always been spirited conversation. I can't help it. I'm a talker. My boredom curdled into aggravation. Upset and uneasy, feeling almost aggressive, I re-entered the room four hours after the meditation had begun.

As soon as I lay back down, Christy held out her hand to me. I took it and accepted this energy. I instantly became aware of a potent, luminous power emanating from Christy's heart to mine. When Christy had healed my back pain on our retreat, it felt as if a butterfly was fluttering up and down my back to heal it. This was completely different: there is no way to describe it other than to say that she cracked my heart open, removed all of its pain, and filled it back up with love and peace.

My anxiety and unrest slowed and washed away until it disappeared completely. I was left with a sensation I had never experienced before. A neutral and all-encompassing sensation of love, which Christy had given to me. As I reflected on this, I knew that my feelings of aggression had been a response to pain, and the many circumstances in my life which have led me to feel I just can't sit in silence. The relief from this ache was so profound, I had to wonder if Christy could teach this process to others. Could we assist people in releasing their own pain?

A few months later, during another visit, an answer came. As we got ready for the day, Christy attempted to open the back door, only to find it locked. It struck her as odd, since our host, the homeowner, had said they preferred the doors to remain unlocked. I, of course, was the culprit.

As a child, my parents had a habit of leaving doors unlocked. In a house as turbulent as mine was, I had to be a little adult in a child's body, pacing through the house after they had gone to sleep, methodically locking every door and window. I told Christy this much, shrugging it off. The genuine irritation on her face made me laugh. Or at least, it did at first. As the day wore on, it became clear that this incident had upset something profound within Christy.

As we delved deeper into her extreme reaction to a simple locked door, we began to realize that it wasn't so simple after all. My action, so clearly tied to the rituals of my own past, had triggered some unresolved issues of Christy's. I had accidentally dredged up old, deeply seated emotions that she hadn't processed.

Christy grabbed a marker and ran to a whiteboard mounted on the wall. After an instant, I grabbed another and joined her. We delved into the idea of triggers: how someone can be intensely affected by a seemingly innocent reminder of a painful memory.

What we had discovered, through the silent meditation and Christy's reaction to the locked door, was that these reactions are hidden within us all. And though they might be buried so deep we can't always recognize them, it's possible to identify and release them. We began to ask questions of ourselves, guided by spirits, and drew out the beginnings of what would become The Process, and your guide to awakening your path.

Chapter 2

Triggers

Now you know the story about how a locked door unlocked the Awakening Your Path method of releasing triggers—The Process. Awakening Your Path is more than just a book: it's a guide to self-awareness that begins with the simplest of moments and unfolds into a powerful methodology. Christy's tale started with a mundane obstacle, but within that uneventful moment lay the catalyst for something extraordinary—the birth of The Process. As she responded to her own triggers, we witnessed the dawn of our collaborative effort to shape and refine The Process into the potent tool it is today. Now we invite you to embark on your own path of self-discovery and growth. So, step into the pages of Awakening Your Path and immerse yourself in a transformative experience guided by the wisdom within. We will be here with you as you travel along your path, ready to support and empower you on your quest for greater self-awareness and fulfillment.

How and why, you may wonder, would such a trivial matter as a locked door set all of this into motion? In fact, what Christy experienced that day is an apt illustration of how we commonly experience triggers and try to dismiss them, as well as how engaging in the emotional and spiritual work of dismantling them can free us to explore new facets of ourselves and our life's purpose.

We were having a working weekend, staying at a residence hosted by someone who rarely locked doors and requested that we not lock the doors. As we were leaving to begin our workday, an unforeseen and harmless obstacle stood in Christy's path: a locked door. When Christy attempted to open the door and realized it was locked, she casually remarked on this unexpected occurrence. She didn't attach much significance to it, until Iris nonchalantly admitted that she had been the one to lock the door. On the surface, it seemed like a minor inconvenience—all Christy had to do was unlock the door and continue on her way.

Instead, this seemingly routine act of leaving a residence triggered an unexpected emotional turmoil within Christy. She found herself caught in a web of emotions, prompting her to delve deeper into the root causes of her heightened emotional state. This maelstrom of feelings took her by surprise. Annoyance surged within her like an unbidden tidal wave. She grappled with an inner commotion, her thoughts incessantly circling around a singular question: who was Iris to disregard the homeowner's explicit wishes and lock the door?

Typically, Christy has a knack for letting such matters slide, quickly processing them and moving forward. After all, she had spent an extended period of time traveling with Iris, growing accustomed to her vigilant behavior, which included incessantly checking doors and ensuring everyone's safety.

This time, things were different. Something about the circumstances of this particular instance had triggered a reaction in Christy that she had never experienced before. In our previous shared adventures, we had invariably found ourselves in unfamiliar places, staying in accommodations unrelated to anyone we knew. In such circumstances, Christy never felt as though anyone's wishes were being disregarded. However, in this instance, we were residing in someone else's home, a space that did not belong to Iris, and that was the crux of the matter.

Christy's disquiet stemmed from the stark reality that Iris was, in essence, overriding the homeowner's preferences. It is essential to underscore the homeowner was utterly unconcerned about Iris's actions. Nevertheless, Christy was struggling to move past her annoyance and get her mind on her work that day.

Consider a second significant factor at play here—Christy's conscious effort to suppress her feelings and rationalize her annoyance. She was fully aware there was no valid reason for her irritations, since Iris's behavior was not intended to be hurtful. Christy managed to discern this was more about her own interpretation of Iris's actions than about Iris herself. As part of the spiritual work Christy was doing that weekend, she had been advised by spirit—her team on the other side, so to speak—to express her true feelings and stand in her truth, speaking up about her emotions. Her own meditations had also led her to understand that she needed to speak her truth that weekend.

And then Christy found herself grappling with an unfamiliar and profound emotional reaction. Spirit persistently urged her to address the issue. Christy considered it absurd to voice her concerns because she believed it was solely her own reaction that was the issue, and Iris's actions were completely inconsequential. What Christy failed to grasp at that moment was this was a multifaceted event. Christy's speaking up not only allowed her to address a trigger, but also allowed Iris to address one.

The persistent nudging from spirit could not be ignored. When Christy finally broached the subject, we recognized it was the beginning of a more profound conversation. We realized that typically, actions like Iris locking a door didn't bother Christy in the least. This realization prompted the development of a series of questions aimed at unraveling and releasing emotional triggers. Not only did this process address Christy's immediate emotional response to Iris's actions, but it also allowed us to explore why Iris consistently felt overly concerned about matters of safety.

Since that day, the original questions that were crafted have undergone continuous, meticulous refinement to forge the most efficient approach to releasing triggers. As you begin to explore your path of releasing triggers, you will gradually unveil layers, revealing further triggers. As each successive layer is dissipated, you experience a heightened sense of lightness, serenity, and an enhanced capacity to navigate your life path with renewed confidence and a profound sense of joy. Instead of feeling powerless in the face of circumstances coming your way, you begin to feel empowered, knowing you have the ability to face any situation you encounter.

Readying yourself to do the work of releasing triggers is an essential step in the process. Without this readiness, despite earnest engagement in the steps to address the trigger, achieving complete release may remain elusive, possibly necessitating multiple walk-throughs of The Process. However, even in a state of unreadiness, engaging in The Process serves a valuable purpose by fostering heightened awareness of the underlying issue. Indeed, the more light we bring to such issues, the greater the potential for healing and joy.

What Is a Trigger?

As we embark on this adventure of self-awareness, let's commence by delving into some of the fundamental concepts and terminology, starting with the term "trigger." In simple terms, a trigger can be thought of as something that makes a person react strongly, even when the situation doesn't seem to warrant it. When someone experiences a trigger, their reaction can be surprising to those around them because it seems to come out of nowhere and be disproportionate to the event.

Another term associated with triggers is "shadow work." Shadow work, a concept introduced by the renowned Swiss psychologist Carl Jung, entails delving into ones "shadow self"—those facets of our personality that we often keep concealed or remain oblivious to in our conscious awareness.

Shadow work necessitates confronting elements of yourself you might instinctively wish to overlook, such as traits like selfishness, greed, anger, or jealousy. Whether we want to admit it to ourselves or not, all of us are capable of such emotions. Jung posited that the process of recognizing and embracing our shadow is essential for achieving a sense of completeness and wholeness as individuals. Embarking on this transformative path allows people to gain profound insights into why certain situations trigger them, and it sheds light on the origins of actions that are found to be less than admirable. This process can be a pivotal part of personal growth, fostering greater self-awareness and an improved understanding of the intricacies of your own psyche.

The Cambridge Dictionary defines triggers as "to cause a strong emotional reaction of fear, shock, anger, or worry in someone, especially because they are made to remember something bad that has happened in the past." As you can tell from this definition, triggers and shadow work sound remarkably alike. However, for the purposes of this writing, we will be using the term "trigger" as opposed to "shadow work."

Like many people, you may feel you have no triggers. Regardless of how spiritually and emotionally evolved you may believe yourself to be or how well you think you've managed your triggers, we invite you to continue reading. We all carry emotional burdens and scars that can be triggered without our conscious awareness. It's important to remember that even if someone has developed the skill to conceal emotional outbursts or suppress inappropriate reactions, it doesn't necessarily mean they have effectively dealt with and processed their triggers in a way that promotes emotional well-being.

We will delve deeper into the topic of recognizing triggers in a later section of this chapter in which we provide a broad overview to give you an idea of what triggers are, how to recognize them, and why releasing them can be transformative. Entire books have been written on triggers, so we don't intend to present a detailed deep dive into triggers here.

We will be focusing on two main categories: internal triggers, which come from within a person, and external triggers, which come from the world around the person experiencing the trigger.

Internal Triggers

Internal triggers encompass a spectrum of thoughts, memories, or emotions that are capable of inciting profound psychological responses. How readily a person may be triggered in this way can be influenced by their other prevailing emotional states, such as feelings of hunger, anger, loneliness, or fatigue. This explains why a particular event may elicit a strong reaction from someone one moment while leaving them unaffected in another. The most recognizable way to realize you are experiencing an internal trigger is the experience of intrusive thoughts.

Intrusive thoughts can be likened to uninvited guests in the vast chambers of the mind, frequently arriving unannounced and carrying with them an unsettling wave of anxiety. With an uncanny ability to disrupt the natural flow of one's thoughts, they make their presence felt, often when least expected. These unwelcome visitors have a knack for slipping through the mental door and initiating a relentless cycle of inner dialogue, which tends to be riddled with self-criticism and doubt. It's crucial to bear in mind this self-critique is frequently groundless, yet our minds persist in traversing the disquieting path, leaving us caught in the grip of their discouraging influence.

We usually feel helpless when faced with negative and intrusive thoughts. And while thoughts can also create negative emotions, it is essential to recognize intrusive thoughts are, at their core, just thoughts—and thoughts can be managed and overcome.

External Triggers

While internal triggers originate from within an individual, external triggers are external factors and situations in a person's surroundings that possess the power to elicit emotional responses. While it is feasible to reduce exposure to certain external triggers through heightened awareness—a coping mechanism we often employ—it is often impractical, if not impossible, to completely evade them, given we must engage with life in all its complexity. External triggers encompass a diverse spectrum of elements including people, places, objects, sensations, and circumstances, each of which has the potential to stir a variety of emotional reactions. Recognizing this is the first step in navigating the intricate interplay between our inner worlds and the external forces that shape our experiences.

For instance, you may have specific people in your life who tend to trigger distressing emotions. While you can take steps to minimize your interactions with them, complete avoidance may not always be viable. Certain places, such as a childhood home filled with unsettling memories, can be particularly distressing and act as a potent trigger. Moreover, everyday items can unexpectedly evoke strong emotional responses in individuals. Merely seeing an alcoholic beverage, for example, may recall memories of an abusive alcoholic parent or partner.

Situations, likewise, can wield significant triggering power. When current circumstances echo past situations linked to negative experiences, encountering a similar scenario can evoke memories of those past events.

It's crucial to approach these triggers with self-compassion and understanding, recognizing them as intrinsic components of human emotions and experiences.

Cognitive Aspects of Experiencing a Triggering Event

When someone experiences a triggering event, whether it stems from their inner feelings or external circumstances, the amygdala, which plays a key role in managing emotions and instinctual reactions, becomes activated. At the same time, the frontal lobe, responsible for higher-level cognitive functions and decision making, becomes less engaged. This means you may already be reacting to a trigger before you even consciously realize it.

Understanding the intricate interplay between various brain regions is essential when delving into the complex dynamics of trauma's impact on both the mind and body. In this context, several key areas of the brain come to the forefront, each playing a pivotal role in shaping our response to traumatic experiences.

At the core of the cerebral function lies the cerebral cortex, particularly the prefrontal cortex. This area, accountable for advanced cognitive functions and decision-making, holds a pivotal position in analyzing and deciphering the impacts of trauma. It strives to comprehend the profound emotions and physiological responses that trauma can trigger.

Delving deeper into the brain's inner sanctum, we encounter the limbic system, an integral component situated at the core of our neural architecture. The limbic system acts as an emotional compass, navigating the tumultuous sea of feelings that accompany traumatic events. Within this network, the amygdala takes center stage. When a person undergoes a traumatic episode, adrenaline surges through the body, and the amygdala becomes the repository of intense emotions and impulsive reactions. It imprints the emotional significance of the event, etching the memory into our consciousness.

The amygdala's role is pivotal as it encapsulates not only the intensity of our emotional response but also the impulsiveness that often accompanies such experiences. In doing so, it contributes to the multi-faceted tapestry of how we perceive, process, and ultimately, heal from

HYPOTHALAMUS

PREFRONTAL CORTEX

PITUARY GLAND

AMYGDALA

CEREBELLUM

BRAIN STEM

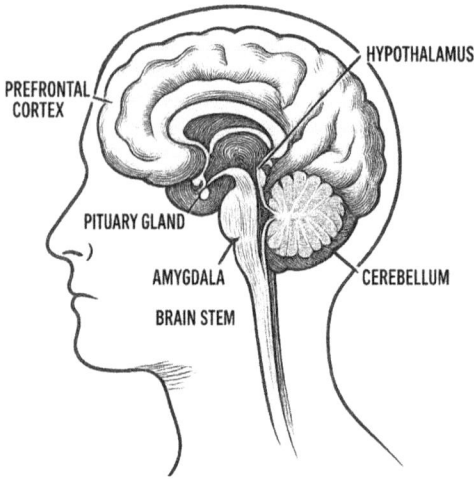

traumatic events. Understanding these neurological nuances brings us closer to comprehending the profound impact of trauma on the human psyche and underscores the importance of compassion and support to those who have endured such experiences.

Following a traumatic experience, the human brain can become exceptionally sensitive to sensory stimuli, often misinterpreting innocuous situations as potentially perilous. Take fireworks, for instance. Instead of perceiving them as beautiful and enjoying them at a time of celebration as they are intended on the 4th of July, they can trigger a negative emotional response for those who have experienced combat. Similarly, the smell of a certain cologne can be triggering for an abuse victim whose abuser wore that same scent.

In this state, the fragments of sensory input are prone to misinterpretation, rendering the brain incapable of distinguishing between actual threats and everyday circumstances. This occurs because the prefrontal cortex, the region of our brain responsible for rational thought, consciousness, information processing, and language comprehension, tends to shut down in response to trauma. As a result, individuals find themselves in a fight, flight, or freeze response mode, which leads to a state of disarray and overwhelm within the brain.

This disorganization in the brain coincides with the body's shift into survival mode, causing the higher cognitive functions and linguistic capabilities housed in the prefrontal cortex to temporarily shut down. The consequence is a deeply ingrained stress response that can have profound and lasting effects.

This course of events may make it difficult to maintain a clear and rational perspective. Instead, the person affected may enter a state driven by instincts and emotions. For those trying to make significant life changes, encountering such triggers can pose substantial challenges to continuing their progress. Therefore, it is crucial to prioritize self-care and be proactive in safeguarding against potential triggers while simultaneously working on releasing and deactivating triggers.

While it is important to take measures to protect oneself from potential triggers when feasible, it is essential to acknowledge that complete avoidance of all triggering situations may not be a realistic goal. Even if we are equipped with an acute awareness of the various stimuli that could elicit distress—be it specific sites, odors, sounds, or other sensory inputs—exerting absolute control over our environment to guarantee an absence of these stimulating elements is insurmountable. Too many external factors, such as unexpected noises or sounds akin to gunfire, like a backfiring car, surprise us despite our best intentions to shield ourselves from such experiences. Even something as seemingly innocuous as the presence of a dog can serve as a source of distress for a person who carries the traumatic memory of a childhood dog bite. Walking by someone in a store who wears a similar cologne to the one worn by your second-grade teacher who called you "dumb" can make you instantly feel small, insignificant, and angry. Recognizing the inevitability of encountering triggers, we must approach this challenge with empathy and understanding, both for ourselves and for those around us who may be grappling with similar vulnerabilities.

Triggers Are a Universal Human Experience

Everyone has triggers of some sort. Even those who feel as if they have no triggers can have them. In our experience, some people who do not recognize they have triggers are actually extremely clairsentient. "Clairsentience," which means "clear feeling," lets you know when something is not quite right. We have worked with several people who at first said they did not have triggers; in truth they instantly felt their clairsentience warn them that they do not like a specific situation or something that is going on, so they distance themselves from the situation. As with people who have become adept at tamping down their emotions, in the short term, both coping mechanisms can be effective, but no real personal growth is made unless the trigger is addressed and released.

In a workshop, a woman, who we will call Carol, had a remarkable clairsentient ability that provided an illustrative example. When queried about releasing triggers, she claimed to have none. We anticipated Carol's response, which is why we wanted to work with her to delve more deeply. Through a series of questions, we uncovered a recent triggering incident: an encounter with someone afflicted by an illness that occasionally caused them to exhibit aggression. Carol confessed to avoiding gatherings and places where this person might be present, even altering her route to evade potential encounters in hallways.

After responding to a series of questions, Carol recalled an incident at a church event where a girl had unexpectedly jumped on Carol and started choking her. Despite Carol's history of enduring bullying, which she believed she had coped with effectively, this event had remained stored in her memory as a trigger. This is where the ego comes into play, with its primary function being self-protection. Carol's ego had preserved these core memories as a defense mechanism. Consequently, whenever she encountered aggression, her unconscious self would activate, prompting her to avoid such situations as a means of protection.

We focused on releasing Carol's trigger, liberating her from the instinctive response of avoiding confrontation. When addressing triggers, it's vitally important to revisit the earliest memory that comes to mind. Sometimes, you may release a trigger that you're aware of without realizing there's an even earlier one. And that's perfectly fine! Using The Process, you address the triggers you're conscious of, and if you find yourself triggered again, you revisit The Process until you're no longer affected. Self-compassion and acknowledging your progress are the keys to success!

We have encountered many people such as Carol who, because they do not feel a huge rush of emotion but rather remove themselves from the situation, feel they have not been triggered. However, being severed from the depths of your emotions can have a profound and potentially devastating impact on your personal life and relationships. Closing off emotions can cast a shadow over your confidence, self-awareness, and your ability to interact and communicate effectively with others, whether you realize it or not.

Often this disassociation is not a deliberate choice, but an involuntary reflex that emerges in response to trauma or distress—incidents that have left incredible imprints within you. This emotional detachment becomes a kind of somber body memory, crystallized by your mind's struggle to grapple with emotions during a turbulent period.

Consider, for instance, an earlier chapter in your life when you found yourself ill equipped to handle a distressing episode—perhaps prolonged spells of neglect and solitude during your childhood, physical or sexual abuse, a sudden loss, or harrowing spectacles you witnessed. Or this emotional shutdown may be rooted in the anxiety, aggression, or turmoil that pervaded your family environment in your formative years. In these tumultuous circumstances, your emotions don't bow to your conscious will. Your brain, besieged with overwhelming sensations, adopts a defensive stance by stifling the pain and powerlessness that emerged during these trying times. Consequently, you find yourself grappling with a pervasive emptiness or an unshakable sense of foreboding. Slowly but surely, your enthusiasm for life wanes, and the things that once ignited your soul with joy and wonder lose their luster.

In the midst of this emotional fog, you might internalize your frustrations and anger, all the while wrestling with a nameless dread. You can become imprisoned by these pent-up emotions, and you begin avoiding challenging situations and interpersonal confrontations. The emotions, when they finally surface, manifest as sporadic bursts of rage or withdrawal, pushed to the forefront only when they become unbearable. It becomes increasingly challenging for friends and family to engage with you, as you drift further into emotional detachment. Loved ones may perceive you as cold and aloof.

Why Release Triggers?

In recent years, psychologists have delved into the complicated workings of our emotional responses, uncovering a profound truth that suppressing or disregarding the negative emotions arising when we're emotionally triggered is an ineffective strategy. Such attempts to stifle these emotions often leave us with physical signs of distress, like sweaty palms and a racing heart. Inevitably, stifled emotions only stay stifled for a certain amount of time and can explode as anger directed at others. It's when we allow ourselves to feel these emotions and then engage in the process of cognitive reappraisal that we begin to experience a remarkable shift towards tranquility.

When we go through a harrowing experience of trauma, our brains encode into our memories not just the raw events, but also this sensory detail surrounding the events. Subsequently, when we stumble upon these sensory cues years later, our brains can reignite the emotional responses linked to that traumatic event. This revival of past feelings can sometimes occur without us consciously comprehending why we are suddenly engulfed in fear or distress. If you were taught by someone in your family or even society in general that it is unacceptable to show these emotions, then you learn to tamp them down or disassociate from them, not act on them.

We may think an event we experience had no impact on us, and when someone triggers us later, we do not even recognize it as a trigger. For instance, consider a scenario where you are involved in a severe car accident. At the time of the accident, you were listening to a certain song, wearing a certain cologne, or even on a certain stretch of road that was having construction. Our brain not only records the incident itself, but also the sensory detail surrounding the event, and it creates a trigger without us consciously knowing it. Inexplicably, these seemingly innocuous sensory encounters can be converted into long-term triggers capable of unsettling us for years to come. The site of orange cones signaling road construction can put us in a cold sweat or hearing the song that was playing at the time of the accident will cause tremendous fear years later.

It is necessary to recognize that trauma is a profoundly individualized experience, and it impacts each person in a unique way. Remarkably, the same traumatic incident may provoke entirely different reactions in two different people. While one person might eventually come to terms with a distressing encounter and move towards acceptance, another person could develop post-traumatic stress disorder in response to the same event.

This divergence in responses can be attributed to a multitude of contrib- uting factors. The impact of a traumatic event on each person hinges on multiple variables, including their inherent personality traits, their social cultural background, the specific attributes of the traumatic incident, the stage of their emotional involvement, and the personal significance they attach to the trauma. All these elements combine to shape the intricate and diverse ways in which we react to trauma.

The ordeal of being emotionally triggered is rarely a pleasant one. Whether we react by succumbing to anger, withdrawing into ourselves, or drowning in a deluge of self-criticism, the consequences weigh heavily on us and those closest to us. These reactions hinder the vital connection that fosters healing and assures us that the present need not repeat itself. When we make the conscious effort to reevaluate what is transpiring and to release triggers and emotionally charged responses, the real work begins to happen. Through working The Process and releasing triggers, we grant ourselves the gift of becoming physically calmer and less emotionally reactive, thereby equipping ourselves to better navigate the challenges we face in awakening our paths. By acknowledging and processing our negative feelings, we create an opportunity for growth, emotional balance, and a deeper connection with ourselves and others.

Romantic relationships hold a significant place in our lives, but the concept of a partner extends beyond just romantic connections; it encompasses business partnerships, friendships, and even familial relationships. When your partner in any of these relationships triggers an emotional response in you, it is a common reaction to point the finger at them. We might blame them for causing emotional distress, heightening our anxiety, or impeding our progress. We may even attribute our insecurities, our lack of ambition, career dissatisfaction, or overall unhappiness to their actions. Sometimes, we retaliate with words or actions to shut them down, or withdraw, distancing ourselves, depending on our individual coping mechanisms and defense strategies.

Consider when you communicate by saying, "I felt triggered because of what you said and how you said it." This terminology can come across as quite loaded. This phrasing can inadvertently place the blame for your emotional reaction on the other person, rather than acknowledging the trigger resides within you. To the other person, it might sound as if you are implying they must change themselves in order for you to avoid being triggered, which can be unfair and counterproductive. Owning our responses and processing our own emotions is important work.

Ultimately, understanding and managing your own triggers promotes a healthier and more compassionate dynamic in all your relationships.

If we do not own our responses when we are interacting within these relationships, we can tend to portray ourselves as innocent victims of our partner's cruelty, often neglecting our own role in the situation or how we reacted under emotional distress. We share these narratives with friends, family, coworkers, and therapists, emphasizing how our partner or family member seems to possess the uncanny ability to push our emotional buttons, causing us to behave out of character. This, we insist, is undoubtedly their fault.

However, the pain inflicted by being triggered varies from person to person, typically due to the elevated expectations and aspirations we hold for the loved one to whom we've opened our hearts. When these cherished companions, whether a friend, family member, or romantic partner, unintentionally say or do something that hurts our feelings, the emotional impact is profound. The harder we fall emotionally, the deeper the emotional wound. We must recognize that while the immediate hurt may feel intense, the root of that pain often originates from past experiences and may not be solely caused by the current triggering incident.

Let's consider the difficulty in confronting our own mistakes and lapses in judgement, especially when we feel mistreated by someone else. This difficulty often arises due to our own need to first process our emotions before we can fully let go of our reactive response. On some occasions, it is a matter of sifting through our own feelings before reaching a point of readiness to release the emotional trigger. In other instances, accepting responsibility for our role in a particular interpersonal interaction can be a daunting task. Human nature sometimes drives us to fixate on the perceived wrongs done to us, effectively casting ourselves as the victims in the narrative.

You have probably seen this type of behavior in your life or that of someone you love, particularly in the context of relationship breakups or divorces, especially when children are involved. In such cases, one partner may have endured inappropriate behavior from their spouse for an extended period. This inadvertently conveyed to their children that the inappropriate behavior is acceptable. Suddenly, the partner decides to end their relationship and seeks support from their children or friends, expecting them to side with them in the breakup because they have now deemed the previously tolerated behavior to be unacceptable.

Whatever the conflict may be, when our loved ones do not immediately align with our perspective, we become frustrated and, without realizing it, slip into victim consciousness. When we feel we are victims, we can react emotionally and manipulatively, trying to sway people to agree with our way of perceiving a situation. Even when it is brought to our attention that our behavior has eroded trust, we may offer a plethora of excuses for our actions. It is undeniably challenging when we feel wronged, and those close to us don't take our side. Nevertheless, it remains our responsibility to manage our emotions in such situations. If we aspire to hold the trust of our family and friends, we must consistently demonstrate trustworthy behavior.

Another scenario wherein we may find ourselves stuck on an emotional roller coaster that we, knowingly or unknowingly, have engineered into our own life is when we become addicted to the tumultuous drama we've woven into our lives. Consider the possibility that when our history is marred by consistently turbulent relationships, we might bear some responsibility for the emotional upheaval that ensues.

It is not uncommon to encounter a person who vehemently declares their aversion to drama, yet curiously, finds themselves embroiled in it on a regular basis. While life on this planet inevitably introduces us to instances of unforeseen turmoil that we played no part in creating, it remains worthwhile to examine whether drama has become such an integral component of our existence that we inadvertently cultivate it.

We all know someone who, whenever others discuss them, the first topic that invariably surfaces in conversation is the drama that seems to trail behind them. Even during casual discussions, the recurring theme is how this person appears to be a magnet for drama wherever they go. However, if you were to engage in a conversation with this very same person, you would likely be told by them that they are among the least dramatic people they know. Drama and emotional turmoil have become such an integral part of their life, they do not even recognize they are a part of its creation.

Releasing triggers can lead to a profound transformation in our emotional landscape, but it may also unearth an unexpected challenge: our addiction to the chaos and drama that have been an integral part of our lives. When you finally let go of a trigger that has been fueling this emotional turmoil and drama, a shift occurs. Suddenly, you find yourself immersed in a state of calm and neutrality. This transition into calm and neutrality is, in fact, the ultimate goal of this process. However, while this newfound state may appear on the surface to be an almost euphoric experience where you are fully in control of your responses in all situations, for those unaccustomed to such tranquility and equilibrium, this shift can initially be misconstrued as a sense of apathy.

In reality, this state of neutrality represents a remarkable achievement, offering rest from the roller coaster of emotions and dramatic ups and downs that plagued your life. The state of neutrality and calm offers a sanctuary where your emotions no longer dictate who you are and your every move. While the initial sensation might be disorienting, it opens the door to a more stable and harmonious existence, where you can make decisions based on reason and clarity of purpose rather than being tossed about by the turbulent currents of emotion. Embracing this newfound equilibrium is a pivotal step in the journey towards a healthier, more balanced, and content life.

The emotional state of neutrality offers a multitude of benefits to us as we navigate life's complexities. By seeking neutrality, we can cultivate a sense of inner calm and equilibrium, allowing us to approach situations with clear eyes and objectivity. This emotional detachment from extremes enables better decision-making, as we can assess circumstances without our judgement being clouded by intense emotions. Neutrality fosters resilience, as it allows us to adapt to challenges with greater ease and to maintain a balanced perspective in both triumphs and setbacks. Furthermore, practicing neutrality promotes healthier relationships, as it encourages empathy and understanding, rather than reacting impulsively based on heightened emotions.

Overall, embracing neutrality empowers us to navigate difficulties with grace while fostering personal growth and enhancing overall well-being. By continually working on releasing triggers, we can reach this state of neutrality.

Iris experienced this exact phenomenon while working on The Process. In one of our working weekends, she became extremely agitated because The Process was not moving along as quickly as she thought it should. Yet, this moment of apparent frustration held within it the seeds of transformation. As she delved deeper into her response to the situation, Iris confronted the emotional trigger that had its origins in her very beginnings, stemming from her time in utero. This emotion had, over the years, grown to become an inseparable companion, a constant presence in her life.

For Iris, her companion was anxiety—a force that had consistently driven her to excel. It had compelled her to meticulously plan for every conceivable scenario, to craft solutions for all potential pitfalls, and to relentlessly push forward. In her perception, anxiety was the potent fuel propelling her towards success. Without its relentless drive, she experienced the strange sense of calm and neutrality mentioned earlier. This sensation of neutrality, paradoxically, felt akin to desolation. The absence of anxiety, in her mind, left a void she struggled to fill.

It was during these challenging moments that Iris reminded herself of her goals and aspirations. In the process of liberating herself from long-held emotional triggers, especially those that had become almost constant due to their lifelong presence, she recognized the initial stages of release could be uncomfortable. The absence of anxiety was unfamiliar and uncharted territory for her, as she had grown accustomed to its influence.

We will address how to navigate this state of calm and neutrality in another chapter in this book. In Iris's case, her experience served as a testament to the complex relationship between each person's past, present, and future. It underscored the necessity of revisiting and refining our goals when we are faced with the challenge of shedding the familiar burdens of emotional triggers. It was a reminder that personal growth often means navigating through the discomfort of change, as well as recognizing the profound impact our emotional histories have on our lives.

Many of us claim our aim is to evade triggers and the accompanying emotional turmoil. We may even assert we are devoid of triggers altogether. However, triggers are universal; we may be able to deny their existence because we possess considerable skill in suppressing our emotions. Nonetheless, we have learned that, usually, the most effective method of averting emotional overwhelm entails confronting triggers and leveraging them as catalysts for personal development. To achieve this delicate equilibrium, it is necessary for each of us to assume responsibility for our own triggers. Christy and Iris wholeheartedly encourage you to continue reading with both an open heart and an open mind. The contents of this book hold invaluable insights, culminating in a guided exploration of the pinnacle—the essence of it all: The Process.

Chapter 3

The Lens Through Which We View the World

Our perception of the world is deeply influenced by our triggers, shaping what philosophers term as our "worldview." This framework serves as a unique and individualized lens, coloring the way we see and interpret the world. It goes beyond mere observation—it plays a pivotal role in guiding our interactions and connections with the world at large and actively shapes our responses, decisions, and the depth of our engagement with the complicated tapestry of existence. Our lens affects the way we move through the world and our lives.

Our understanding of the world around us isn't flawless; it's derived from a complex interplay involving the information we receive through our senses, the memories of our previous encounters, and the biases ingrained in our thinking patterns. Consider a classic optical illusion: an object seemingly gliding diagonally when, in truth, it's moving straight up and down. We don't simply absorb reality as it is; rather, our minds construct a narrative based on the combination of our desires, expectations, and personal history. This narrative significantly influences how we perceive experiences, introducing preconceptions that color our interpretation of the world.

Though philosophers refer to this narrative as our "worldview," here we will refer to this as the lens through which we view life. It is crucial to thoroughly comprehend the immense impact this "lens" has on our lives. It is not merely a passive filter; it actively molds our perception of information and deeply influences how we interpret subtle cues, such as the nuances in people's body language. Consequently, it profoundly shapes our reactions and behaviors in everyday interactions without us consciously realizing it.

Our deeply ingrained beliefs and the way we perceive the world around us are intricately woven together, influencing the very fabric of reality we perceive within our minds. These perceptions, often vivid and deeply convincing, serve as an interpreter through which we understand the world. However, it's vital to recognize this interpreter might not always offer an accurate portrayal of objective reality. It's essential to embrace the idea that our perspectives, however powerful, may not encompass the entirety of truth. They are shaped by our experiences, biases, and limited understanding, potentially veiling the complete picture of reality.

In acknowledging this disparity between our perceptions and objective truth, we grant ourselves the opportunity for growth and understanding. We begin to navigate the world with humility, realizing our beliefs, while deeply held, might not always align with what objectively exists. This realization doesn't diminish the significance of our perceptions, but instead encourages a more open-minded approach to interpreting the world. By understanding the potential disparity between our perceived reality and objective truth, we foster empathy, curiosity, and a willingness to explore alternative perspectives. It is a profound recognition that, while our beliefs hold great power, they are not without flaws. Embracing this truth enables us to engage more genuinely with the diverse realities that exist beyond our own limited perceptions.

Our lens through which we perceive and interpret the world is not merely shaped by our experiences and beliefs but is also significantly influenced by biases. These biases, often subconscious and ingrained within us, impact how we process information, make decisions, and form opinions about the world around us. They stem from various sources, including cultural, social, cognitive, and personal factors, creating a filter through which we understand reality. Discovering and understanding these biases is crucial, as they can inadvertently skew our perceptions,

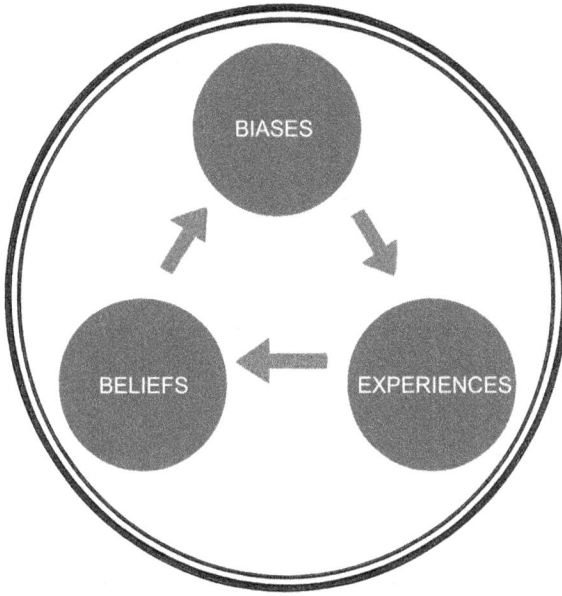

leading to misconceptions, prejudices, and a limited understanding of the complexities within our society and beyond it. This can lead us to react to intentions we think exist, but in reality, are not there at all.

While some biases stand prominently in our awareness, others are deeply ingrained, camouflaged within our subconscious, influencing our judgments without a second thought. These biases, ranging from memory bias, confirmation bias, rosy retrospection bias, and anchoring bias, to implicit biases, to name just a few, are based on social, cultural, or personal experiences. These biases quietly mold our perceptions and interactions. Unearthing and understanding these concealed biases is akin to navigating a labyrinth. Using The Process to find your way through life's maze is challenging yet rewards us through its power to change our own lives in profoundly positive ways. If everyone were to examine their biases, we could all enjoy a more inclusive, informed, and equitable society.

Though we will not delve into all the biases, we will cover a few to give you an understanding of the impact these biases have on our interaction with the world.

Memory Bias

Memory bias is a fascinating phenomenon that shapes the way we recall events from our past. Rather than rigidly preserving exact replicas of reality, our memories are malleable and can undergo a subtle transformation. Cognitive psychologist Gordon Bower aptly describes this process as one of reconstruction, wherein our recollections are not static archives, but fluid impressions subject to alteration and inaccuracy.

It is crucial to understand memory bias encompasses a spectrum of cognitive biases, each with its unique subtleties and effects on our recall. Some of these biases play a positive role, protecting us from distressing memories, while others may exert a less favorable influence, leading us to base decisions on current information rather than older, more relevant data.

Our memories are not mere recordings; they are dynamic entities prone to adaptation and manipulation during the recall process. This interplay of memories and biases underscores the complexity of human memory and how it influences our perceptions and decision making. To add to this intricate interplay, if a memory is stored during a traumatic event, it can be more difficult to recall because the trauma creates time gaps in our memories, and the information is not stored in a linear fashion.

Confirmation Bias

Confirmation bias refers to the tendency of individuals to seek, interpret, or remember information in a way that confirms their preexisting beliefs or hypotheses. It is a cognitive bias that influences how people gather and interpret information, often leading them to favor information supporting their existing views while dismissing or ignoring information that contradicts those beliefs.

Confirmation bias can affect various aspects of life, including decision making, problem solving, and the way we interact with each other. It can reinforce stereotypes, perpetuate misinformation, and hinder the ability to consider alternative perspectives objectively.

This bias occurs because the human brain naturally seeks consistency and affirmation of what it already knows or believes. As a result, we might unknowingly disregard evidence that challenges our beliefs or selectively seek out information aligning with our preconceptions.

Recognizing confirmation bias is essential in critical-thinking and decision-making processes. Being aware of this bias can help us actively seek diverse perspectives, challenge our own assumptions, and make more informed and objective judgments. If you have difficulty releasing a confirmation bias, walking through The Process could lead to discoveries you had never considered before.

Rosy Retrospection Bias

The phenomenon known as rosy retrospection bias reflects our inclination to remember the past in a way that embellishes its positive aspects while downplaying its negatives. It's like viewing the past through a set of rose-tinted glasses, where the memories appear more pleasant and idyllic than they might have been in reality. This bias resonates deeply with the Latin adage memoria praeteritorum bonorum, which translates to "memory of a good past," or more idiomatically as "good old days," emphasizing how we often tend to selectively recall the good parts of our past experiences.

Our minds have a remarkable capacity to highlight the brighter moments of the past, creating a nostalgic glow that can overshadow the challenges and difficulties we might have faced at the time. This tendency to romanticize the past can lead us to believe things were better back then than they are in our current circumstances.

This bias doesn't necessarily mean our memories are inaccurate or false; rather, it highlights how our emotions and perceptions shape the way we remember events. The positive feelings associated with certain memories often become more pronounced over time, contributing to this phenomenon.

It is essential to acknowledge the rosy retrospection bias, as it can influence our decisions and perceptions of the present. Understanding that our recollections might be skewed towards the positive can help us approach nostalgia with a balanced perspective. By recognizing this bias, we can appreciate the beauty of fond memories while also acknowledging the complexities and realities of the past.

Anchoring Bias

Anchoring bias is a thought pattern that heavily influences how we make decisions and form judgments. It emerges when we place excessive reliance on the initial nugget of information we receive, commonly known as the "anchor," while making subsequent estimations or judgments, regardless of the relevance or randomness of this initial input.

Once this anchor is set, we often recalibrate our later conclusions and decisions based on this initial reference point. However, this adjustment tends to lack sufficient reasoning or consideration, leading to conclusions that are inherently biased.

Imagine you're shopping for a new car, and the first dealership you visit offers a vehicle for $35,000. Even though you're just starting to explore your options, that price becomes your reference point, or anchor. As you continue visiting other dealerships, you find a similar car for $32,000. Because you've already anchored the value of the car at $35,000, the $32,000 price seems like a great deal, and you're tempted to buy it. However, in reality, there might be even better deals available, or you might overlook important features that justify a higher price, all because the initial figure you saw influenced your judgment. This is how anchoring bias can affect decision making, causing you to base your choice on the first piece of information you encountered.

The impact of anchoring bias extends across diverse realms of decision making, be it in negotiations, purchase choices, or even self-assessments. Recognizing this bias can empower us to make more informed decisions by consciously examining and critically evaluating the validity of initial anchors before arriving at judgments or estimates. Awareness and conscious consideration can serve as powerful tools to counteract the sway of anchoring bias in decision-making processes, fostering more rational and balanced conclusions.

Consistency Bias

Another common bias we tend to fall victim to is consistency bias. This cognitive bias tricks us into mistakenly assuming our past thoughts and behaviors perfectly align with our present ones. This misconception significantly contributes to fostering a sense of continuity within our self-image.

It's fascinating how this bias plays a considerable role in shaping our perceptions about ourselves. We often tend to overestimate the consistency of our beliefs and actions over time. This overestimation creates within our minds a seamless narrative, leading us to believe that who we were in the past perfectly aligns with who we are in the present.

However, this bias can be misleading. It fails to account for the natural evolution and change which occurs within us as individuals. Human beings are not static—our thoughts, perspectives, and behaviors undergo constant development and alteration as we grow and encounter new experiences.

Recognizing consistency bias helps us acknowledge the fallibility in assuming perfect continuity within our self-image. Embracing the idea of personal growth and change becomes essential in navigating this bias. It allows us to appreciate the complexity of our identity, understanding that while our past shapes us, it does not solely define who we are in the present moment.

Mood-Congruent Memory Bias

Additionally, the mood-congruent memory bias plays a significant role in shaping our recollection process, often highlighting memories that align with our present emotional state. For example, when we experience a sense of calmness, it can prompt the remembrance of serene and peaceful moments from our past. Conversely, feelings of stress tend to evoke memories associated with moments of anxiety and tension. This intricate relationship between our emotions and memory retrieval mechanisms underscores how our current feelings can profoundly influence the types of recollections that come to the forefront of our minds.

Hindsight Bias

Hindsight bias tends to nudge us into believing past events were significantly more predictable than they were. This inclination often creates a feeling as if we had foreseen the outcome all along, despite the true unpredictability of those moments.

Implicit Bias

A strong bias that unconsciously affects our understanding, actions, and decisions towards certain groups of people is implicit bias. This bias is not openly expressed or consciously recognized but exists within our subconscious, shaping our perceptions and behaviors.

It is essential to understand that implicit biases are not indicative of your character or intentional beliefs. Rather, they are formed by a multitude of factors such as cultural upbringing, societal influences, media portrayals, personal experiences, and education. These biases can manifest based on various characteristics like race, gender, age, ethnicity, religion, sexual orientation, and more.

Recognizing and addressing implicit biases requires self-reflection, education, and actively seeking to understand and appreciate diverse perspectives. It involves consciously challenging preconceived notions and being open to learning and unlearning societal conditioning. Releasing the triggers affecting your worldview or lens is imperative to becoming neutral, and it is in this neutrality we can appreciate and learn from people's differences with a compassionate heart.

Egocentric Bias

Furthermore, biases such as the egocentric bias shape the way we recall events, often swaying our memories to align with our self-interest. For instance, this bias might lead us to embellish our exam grades or exaggerate the size of a fish we caught, painting a picture that suits our personal narrative or enhances our image in our own eyes or the eyes of others. These biases play a significant role in shaping our perception of past events and can distort our memories to fit a more favorable or convenient version of reality.

Availability Bias

The availability bias, a common cognitive phenomenon, shapes our perceptions of probability based on the ease of recalling similar occurrences. When vivid memories of specific events come to mind, we tend to overestimate their frequency or likelihood of happening. This mental shortcut often influences our assessments of how probable something is.

However, relying solely on the availability bias can lead to erroneous conclusions. The mere fact that something is more memorable or representative doesn't necessarily make it more probable in reality. Christy has personally grappled with this bias, especially when it comes to air travel. As discussed, our memories are remarkable, but also prone to various influences that alter how we perceive and recall events. In

Christy's Struggle with Availability Bias

Despite knowing the statistical safety of airplanes, I used to struggle with anxiety every time I flew. To assuage my fears, I continually reminded myself of the statistical safety records. Yet, a significant shift occurred when I read a story that described the tragic passing of a loved one in a plane crash. Suddenly, despite my efforts to reinforce the statistical safety of flying, my mind fixated on the vivid image conveyed by the spirit of the departed that showed their tragic demise.

The next time I flew after reading that, though I attempted to reassure myself with the air travel safety data, that image of the spirit's untimely demise overshadowed my attempts at rationality. Thankfully, by this point Iris and I had developed The Process to release triggers. I was able to work The Process while sitting on the plane before we even took off.

This emotionally charged experience has highlighted how the availability bias can persistently influence our perceptions and emotions, despite our conscious efforts to rely on logical reasoning and statistical evidence. Without the ability to release my trigger associated with flying, my travel would have been significantly curtailed.

addition to the biases already mentioned, biases such as the recency effect, choice-supportive bias, and fading-affect bias illustrate how our thoughts can shape and distort our memories. It's how our own personal lens is created. This lens sometimes causes us to see things in a distorted manner. Understanding the influence of these cognitive biases is essential for developing a more accurate and objective interpretation of our experiences.

You do not need to know the definition of each bias or be able to name the one you are experiencing to recognize when these biases are at play—however, being able to recognize that some type of bias is in play is crucial. It is like being aware of our own mental goggles, allowing us to take them off momentarily and see things more objectively. This self-awareness offers a chance to step back, reassess, work The Process discussed in this book, and strive for a more neutral perspective. By acknowledging these influences, we pave the way for a broader, more inclusive understanding of situations. It is about creating room and moving to a point of view that isn't solely colored by our own individual experiences and biases.

As you grow more skilled in the inner work of embracing your emotions and navigating through the transformative journey of personal growth, you'll notice a remarkable shift. This evolution not only enables you to delve deeper into The Process, but also enhances your ability to perceive life with greater clarity and receptivity. This practice cultivates a heightened awareness that enables us to see beyond our preconceptions, unveiling a wealth of hidden information and enriching our understanding of the world around us.

Consider the unexpected revelation when revisiting a photograph and discovering previously unnoticed layers within. Much like this experience, our outlook on the world is shaped by our unique perspectives. Frequently, we're drawn towards what we expect or wish to see, inadvertently overlooking the multitude of details that encompass our focal point. This work is akin to wiping the dust off a lens, allowing previously unseen aspects of life to come into focus.

The intricate workings of our minds resemble fixed lenses, meticulously crafted over time to prioritize the familiar and the comfortable. These lenses wield substantial influence over what we consciously absorb and comprehend. This truth became piercingly clear during a trip Christy took with her husband. Despite the many years she has been married and the multitude of experiences they've shared, the contrasting lenses through which she and her husband individually perceive the world, shaped by their unique backgrounds, upbringings, and career choices, emerged conspicuously into view as she relates here:

"We were walking through Naples, Italy, in-route from our hotel to the train station, when we encountered a disheveled homeless person. In a reflex of compassion, I directed positive energy towards them, sending waves of love and understanding. As I sent this energy towards this homeless gentleman, I saw two spirit guides with him, one on each side standing at parade rest. One of the guides nodded their head at me and said, "We've got him." As I shared what occurred with my husband, he asked about my selective focus on that particular person. My rationale was rooted in the visible signs of substance abuse exhibited by the individual.

In response, my husband smiled gently and drew my attention to the numerous others we had passed engaged in drug use during our previous walks through Naples. Astonishingly, I had not registered their presence. This revelation prompted me to question why my husband hadn't pointed this out earlier. His response was profound: "I knew you hadn't seen them, and there was no reason for you to." He understood that my lens of perception operated differently, filtering out certain aspects that didn't easily align with my accustomed view of the world."

In essence, our unique lenses subtly shape our perceptions, emphasizing what resonates within our established frameworks while unwittingly obscuring elements that fall outside of our usual scope of observation. This revelation gave Christy a deeper understanding of how our individual lenses influence the way we interpret and engage with the world around us, reminding her of the importance of getting to a state of neutrality where we can more easily access empathy, understanding, and the complexities of human perception.

Christy relates her lived experience of how this lens can shape a person's life path in material ways:

"Throughout my life, there was a lens through which I perceived the world, one which significantly influenced my daily existence—a perspective on money that eluded my awareness as a critical issue until well into my adulthood. To say I was raised without financial abundance is an understatement, and from the age of thirteen, I shouldered the responsibility of funding my necessities—clothes, school lunches, and any additional desires beyond a roof over my head.

"After marriage, neither my husband nor I possessed substantial income or the educational foundation required to secure financially rewarding opportunities. Our initial years together were devoid of financial stability, posing a considerable challenge as we navigated life's demands. Eventually, my husband enlisted in the military, which provided a certain level of stability, albeit not a 'good' income, especially given that we already had a child and all the expenses inherent in supporting a growing family. To give you a sense of our situation, even upon my husband's entry into active duty, had we applied for food stamps, we would have met the criteria.

"This background shaped my perception of money in profound ways, embedding a deep-seated consciousness about financial struggles that infiltrated my thoughts and actions daily. The scarcity I experienced during my formative years left an indelible mark, steering my decisions and attitudes towards financial matters. The constant juggling of resources and the weight of financial strain became ingrained, affecting how I approached every aspect of life, from budgeting and saving to opportunities pursued and the aspirations I dared to entertain.

"Recognizing the far-reaching implications of this early experience, I have come to appreciate how it influenced my relationship with money, fostering both resilience and caution in equal measure. It underscored the importance of resourcefulness, instilling a relentless drive to overcome obstacles and ensure the well-being of my family. However, it also instigated a certain hesitancy, a subconscious fear of financial insecurity that at times hindered my willingness to take calculated risks or envision a future unshackled from immediate monetary concerns.

"Even in this moment, I use The Process to cleanse my perspective and reach a state of neutrality when significant business prospects arise. If I hadn't acquired the ability to identify my emotional triggers and let them go, my burgeoning business might not have thrived. My perception of scarcity and lack was deeply rooted within me from an early age. Through recognizing and addressing these tendencies, I've been able to pave the way for my business growth."

Just as our biases and triggers influence our relationship with money, they affect our personal relationships. A lens as simple as how we view others can hold substantial sway over our relationships, whether this is our boss, teacher, parent, or sibling. For instance, if you view them as consistently opposed to you, this perspective could significantly shape your responses while interacting with them. This habitual perception often triggers defensive, combative, or negatively reactive behaviors, fostering a sense of victimhood.

Viewing ourselves as a victim can have a significant negative impact on relationships. We have all at some point fallen into the victimhood mentality, even while perched on our soap box railing against it. Victimhood can affect relationships by causing a communication breakdown, as victims may struggle to effectively communicate their needs, emotions, or viewpoints, leading to misunderstandings or conflicts in relationships. If we are feeling victimized, we might express ourselves in a passive-aggressive manner. Or, we may seek constant validation, support, or reassurance from others, creating a dynamic where we rely heavily on our partners or friends for emotional reinforcement. This can strain relationships as the burden of support becomes overwhelming for our friend or partner. Additionally, victimhood can cause resentment and frustration as the constant focus on our own suffering might make others feel helpless or frustrated due to their inability to provide a lasting solution. It can also lead to an imbalance of power, and the victim may manipulate situations or guilt-trip others to gain control or sympathy, which tips the scales of equality and fairness in the relationship.

Finally, victimhood may lead us down the path of shrugging off responsibility for our actions or choices, attributing negative outcomes solely to external factors or other people. This lack of accountability can strain relationships by preventing growth or resolution of conflicts. Constant victimhood can erode trust in relationships. If you are taking a role as a victim, others might perceive you as manipulative or insincere, making it challenging to build or maintain trust.

This outlook, constantly perceiving others as adversaries and adopting a victimhood mentality, can pave the path towards profound unhappiness and upheaval both within yourself and in external interactions.

Conversely, perceiving people through a more positive lens tends to cultivate elevated levels of joy and inner peace. This shift in perception can foster healthier, more harmonious relationships by encouraging a sense of connection and understanding rather than conflict and discord. Learning to view people and situations with a clean lens allows us to live fuller, more productive lives.

It is important to note that being a victim of a genuine injustice or trauma is entirely different from adopting a victim mentality as a personality trait. Addressing genuine pain or trauma through appropriate channels is essential for healing. However, adopting a victim mentality as a habitual way of interacting with the world can significantly impact relationships. Healthy relationships thrive on mutual respect, empathy, communication, and support.

We have witnessed clients experiencing profound shifts in their perspectives and emotional triggers using The Process as a transformative process. This process often leads them to perceive situations in an entirely new light, uncovering information and processing data that had previously eluded them. It is a journey that sometimes demands deep introspection, prompting us to take responsibility and offer apologies to those we may have unknowingly hurt.

Conversely, this newfound awareness might also compel us to establish boundaries with others with whom we had not felt the need to set limits before. This is a natural consequence of this growth, as we begin to prioritize our emotional well-being and honor our own needs in a way we might not have previously considered.

Navigating Your Path

Embarking on the transformative path guided by The Process sparks a multitude of challenges that might seem insurmountable and intimidating. It's completely understandable to feel overwhelmed at times. However, remember that facing difficulty does not define your capabilities. You possess the strength to overcome obstacles, even the toughest ones. You can do hard things!

The path to personal transformation often entails moments that test your resilience and determination. While these challenges may be tough, they are not beyond your capacity to navigate. Despite the trials and tribulations along the way, your journey towards personal growth is a testament to your self-worth. You are inherently deserving of the effort it takes to evolve into a happier, more serene, joyful, and compassionate version of yourself. It is a testament to your commitment to embracing a life resonating with inner peace and fulfillment. Know that the effort you put into this transformative process is an investment in your own well-being and contentment. You are capable, worthy, and deserving of the positive changes that come from this introspective work.

You should also know that it is normal for your participation with The Process to fluctuate. There will be days where you will find yourself not utilizing it at all, as well as days where you will engage in it multiple times. Both instances represent progress on awakening your path. These fluctuations serve as reminders of the dynamic nature of your growth and your ongoing commitment to self-awareness and personal development.

Seeking a fresh outlook on the world is a complex journey which necessitates not only patience, but also a gentle, nurturing attitude towards yourself. Actively reshaping how you perceive reality involves self-compassion amidst the fluctuations and setbacks along your path. There will undoubtedly be days when you will employ techniques to release a trigger, only to find it resurfacing once more. It's essential to approach these instances with kindness and understanding. Such moments often signify the trigger was not wholly resolved during its initial release. Simply reengaging with The Process can aid in its resolution.

Awakening and navigating your path, as with any kind of transformation, demands a genuine openness to change. Many times, we express a strong wish to improve various aspects of our lives, yet we often lack the genuine readiness required to put these changes into action. Holding a sincere desire to see things differently plays a pivotal role in your path towards transformation. Mental preparedness to confront change creates an environment conducive to learning, enabling the development of new perspectives and the release of triggers.

Resistance to change often stems from a deeply ingrained human instinct to seek comfort and familiarity. Even when faced with the prospect of improvement or betterment, we may hesitate to embrace change simply because we find solace in the known. This inclination towards the familiar is a psychological defense mechanism, guiding us towards a sense of security and stability in an otherwise uncertain world. Whether it's sticking to traditional routines, familiar environments, or established patterns of behavior, we often cling to what we know, even if it means sacrificing potential growth or progress.

Because of our fear of the unknown, stepping into unfamiliar territory can be daunting, triggering feelings of anxiety and apprehension. We may worry about the potential risks and uncertainties associated with change, preferring the predictability of our current circumstances, even if we recognize those circumstances may not be optimal. This aversion to stepping outside our comfort zone can lead us to resist change, despite the potential benefits it may offer. Thus, while change may be necessary for personal or professional development, the allure of familiarity often prevails, making it challenging for us to welcome new opportunities for growth and improvement.

In our daily lives, we often find ourselves deeply entrenched in our accustomed ways of perceiving things, which can make it challenging to identify our blind spots. It's perfectly natural to view situations through a particular lens shaped by our experiences, beliefs, and upbringing. However, this habitual way of seeing things might occasionally prevent us from grasping a more favorable or accurate perspective.

During such moments, it becomes immensely beneficial to seek an external viewpoint. Whether it's seeking counsel from a trusted friend, confiding in a family member, or consulting a professional like a psychologist, engaging in conversations with others can offer invaluable fresh insights. These supporters and confidants possess the ability to shed light on alternative viewpoints that might have eluded us previously, thereby broadening our understanding and perception of a situation.

When we encounter an unfamiliar viewpoint that challenges our usual perspective, it is essential to give it a chance to settle within us. Paying attention to how it resonates with our inner feelings and thoughts is crucial. If the new viewpoint feels discordant or triggers an emotional response within us, it serves as a significant signal to initiate The Process.

The Process isn't intended to criticize or invalidate our existing perceptions. Rather, it is an opportunity for enrichment and refinement. By welcoming diverse perspectives, we create fertile ground for personal growth and development. Embracing these discussions enables us to elevate our perceptions and minimize potential errors in our judgments.

Ultimately, staying open to alternative viewpoints is fundamental to continually improving our understanding of the complex world surrounding us. It is not merely about rectifying flaws in our perceptions, but about evolving towards a more nuanced and comprehensive understanding of the multifaceted aspects of life.

One of the greatest challenges to growth lies in our inability to transcend our biases and genuinely comprehend alternative viewpoints. We may feel defensive and want validation for our viewpoint, which can cause us to fall into the trap of preparing counterarguments instead of fully listening to what others are expressing. This tendency hinders authentic dialogue, preventing us from truly grasping the essence of differing perspectives and perpetuating the cycle of discord.

In moments when you sense a surge of emotions stirred by someone, something, or a particular situation, consider the profound impact of hitting the "pause button." Though change might feel uncomfortable in the beginning, the space to breathe and ground yourself in the present moment is well worth the effort. Taking this breath provides the opportunity to swiftly engage in The Process, fostering a quick shift to a neutral state. Practicing The Process takes time, yet it empowers you to consciously choose your response, emerging from a place of inner strength.

At times, a quick run-through of The Process may not be sufficient to alter your perspective, if the trigger is deeply ingrained. In such cases, allowing yourself a "grownup time-out" is not just acceptable but a commendable act of self-care. It is okay to communicate your need to process things to those involved, assuring them that you'll address the matter with them at a more appropriate time. This action honors your emotional well-being and demonstrates a mature approach to resolving conflicts or challenges. This time-out grants you the space necessary to engage in The Process in a more thorough and detailed manner.

Within each of us lies an array of unique perceptions shaping how we interpret the world. Acknowledging and understanding these individual patterns is essential for freeing ourselves from their constraints. Consider this: if impartial observers, devoid of personal biases, were faced with a situation similar to yours, would they draw the same conclusions? If uncertain, there's no harm in running through The Process.

Engaging in this practice cultivates a heightened level of critical thinking, enabling us to distance ourselves from emotional biases. This deliberate step allows us to uncover elements that might have initially evaded notice due to our immersion in our own patterns of thinking.

This method isn't merely about analysis; it's a potent tool for fostering self-awareness and personal development. It empowers you to widen your perspectives, capturing insights that might have otherwise slipped by unnoticed. By encouraging you to transcend your ingrained inclinations, it facilitates a deeper and more comprehensive understanding of diverse situations. This, in turn, enhances your capacity to navigate life's complexities with clarity and objectivity. Ultimately, this approach serves as a pathway towards growth and a more profound connection with the world around you.

The Domino Effect of Self-Evolution: Beyond Personal Change

Throughout this transformative expedition, you might notice shifts in your reactions, or perhaps a lack thereof, which could potentially unsettle those around you. It is crucial to approach these reactions from others with compassionate understanding. Recognize that your personal growth might challenge or surprise others, which highlights the need for empathy in navigating these interactions. Your journey towards personal growth holds the power to ignite change, not only within yourself but also within the dynamics of the relationships you share with others. This is a testament to the profound impact self-evolution can have on the world around us.

Our perceptions and predispositions serve as powerful filters, subtly shaping every facet of our thoughts, actions, and responses. Whether consciously acknowledged or not, these lenses heavily influence our perspectives on an array of subjects spanning religion, parenthood, finances, social welfare, dietary choices, residential preferences, the value of higher education, vehicle preferences, and more. Consider, for instance, the way our beliefs about religion dictate our moral compass or how our views on parenting influence our approach to nurturing the next generation. Even seemingly unrelated decisions such as our stance on social programs or our food choices can be traced back to the lens through which we perceive the world.

The collective impact of these personal biases extends beyond individual choices; it permeates our familial dynamics, shapes the fabric of our communities, influences governance in cities and nations, and profoundly shapes the stance of political parties. Regrettably, the failure to step outside our own perspectives has resulted in fractures within families, divisions within societies, and a lack of cohesion within governing bodies.

Imagine being invited by a dear friend, someone whose company you cherish, to join an outing with a group of individuals who, at first glance, seem drastically different from you. This initial observation might trigger a concern you won't find common ground or enjoy yourself among these contrasting personalities.

However, while it is natural to gravitate towards those who share your perspectives and values, it is equally important to embrace diversity in social circles. Engaging with people who hold different beliefs or come from varied backgrounds is an opportunity for personal growth. It allows you to broaden your perspectives, challenge preconceived notions, and gain a deeper understanding of the world.

When we exclusively surround ourselves with like-minded individuals, we risk becoming entrenched in our own viewpoints. This insularity can lead to a narrowed vision, clouded by our biases and assumptions. We might inadvertently believe our perspective is the only valid one, dismissing alternative viewpoints as incorrect or inferior. This can hurt our relationships and ultimately, our healing process.

By venturing beyond our comfort zones and interacting with diverse groups, we clear the fog from our lenses. Engaging with people of varied experiences helps us appreciate different angles of truth. It fosters empathy, tolerance, and a more comprehensive understanding of humanity.

Therefore, while it may seem daunting to spend time with those who appear different, it is an invaluable opportunity for personal development. Embracing diversity enriches our lives, offering an array of perspectives that ultimately enhances our empathy, knowledge, and appreciation for the rich tapestry of human existence.

The more we expand our connections to the world, the more opportunities we have to ask ourselves—through what lens do I choose to perceive it? Proust, the French novelist, said the following about art. It was his belief art was the best way to see through another lens:

"A pair of wings, a different respiratory system, which enabled us to travel through space, would in no way help us, for if we visited Mars or Venus while keeping the same senses, they would clothe everything we could see in the same aspect as the things of the Earth. The only true voyage, the only bath in the Fountain of Youth, would be not to visit strange lands but to possess other eyes, to see the universe through the eyes of another, of a hundred others, to see the universes that each of them sees, that each of them is; and this we do, with great artists; with artists like these we really fly from star to star."

In our personal belief, the most genuine and unclouded way to perceive the world is through the lens of love. It is not about adopting the perspectives imposed by our religious teachings, familial influences, societal norms, or cultural expectations—those may not truly be your own vision. Those lenses often distort our vision, shaping our perceptions in ways that might not resonate with our authentic selves.

When we see the world solely through the perspectives of others, it is like looking through a skewed and imperfect lens. But when we choose love as our guiding principle, it brings clarity and understanding. It allows us to approach life with empathy, compassion, and kindness towards everyone around us.

To fully embody this love-based perspective, we must first free ourselves from the triggers and biases that hinder our ability to connect on a deeper level. It is about tapping into the boundless capacity for unconditional love that resides within each of us. Yes, every single one of us holds this potential, irrespective of our religious upbringing, social class, race, or even whether we actively pursue this potential or not. As you begin to unfold your personal vision and potential, you will find that you begin to send waves of change throughout your sphere of influence. Indeed, as we change, the world changes with us.

We want to emphasize there is not a single prescribed method you can use to achieve this state of being. While we don't assert The Process is the exclusive way to advance along your path, we acknowledge that if you are drawn to this book, it can serve as a valuable tool in your personal toolbox towards awakening your path. It might offer guidance and support in your quest to embrace and embody love as your primary lens through which you perceive and interact with the world.

While we've shared some instances demonstrating how The Process aids in releasing triggers, enabling a more efficient evaluation of incoming data, it is essential to understand this journey demands diligence, effort, and a genuine desire for personal growth. Information inundates us from a myriad of sources—through body language, subtle facial expressions, word selection, tonal nuances, internal responses, or environmental cues, to name a few. Self-improvement is a lifelong endeavor, necessitating consistent dedication. Yet, it is a path well within your capabilities. Remember, investing in your growth and development is a testament to your inherent worthiness. You deserve to become the best version of yourself!

Chapter 4

Awareness & Self-Reflection

In exploring the essence of our being, we delve into the complex interplay between the desires of our individual souls and the pervasive influence of our conditioning. Our soul's composition is as diverse as people are; our soul is a dynamic entity shaped by the ebb and flow of energies that permeate our existence. We exist as vibrant, energetic beings, perpetually attuned to the frequencies that surround us, shaping and reshaping our inner landscapes. We experience our lives like a river's current— ever-shifting, reflecting the elaborate dance between our inner selves and the external stimuli we encounter.

You may experience the conflict between your soul's desires and your conditioning as a sensation that grips your soul, like a melody that refuses to harmonize. It's not just a fleeting discomfort; it's a persistent disquiet that haunts your nights and casts long shadows over your days. There's a constant tug-of-war within you, a battle between the person you are and the person your soul truly aspires to be. As you begin the work of aligning your outer self with your true self, your inner pendulum may swing erratically, oscillating between rebellion and resignation. It may seem that for every triumph, there is an equal and opposite sense of disillusionment. However, in the midst of this turmoil, the allure of escaping the confines of societal norms will grow increasingly tempting—a tantalizing alternative to the relentless pursuit of an unattainable ideal projected onto you by others.

Embracing Incongruence: the Gateway to Self-Discovery

A soul's life theme can be likened to an energetic quality, shaped by past choices and experiences. Consider, for instance, the varied life themes of abundance, acceptance, trust, passion, and partnership, among others. If your primary life theme is "happiness," you might find yourself continually drawn to explore activities, relationships, and experiences that evoke joy and fulfillment. Similarly, someone whose primary life theme is "abundance" may traverse the spectrum from financial wealth to abundance in love, wisdom, creativity, and more.

At the core of our existence lies the dynamic essence of our soul, a complex entity sculpted by our experiences. We are in constant energetic resonance with the frequencies that surround us, shaping our thoughts, emotions, and actions. Just as no two fingerprints are alike, the imprint of each soul is uniquely crafted, reflecting the kaleidoscope of encounters and interactions it has traversed.

Understanding energy is crucial to comprehending both ourselves and our interactions with the world around us. "Energy" refers not only to physical energy but also emotional, mental, and spiritual energies. Our beings are comprised of various energies, continually fluctuating and interacting with one another. These energies are influenced by our thoughts, emotions, beliefs, experiences, and the energies present in our environment.

Conditioning, too, can be viewed as a form of energy. It encompasses the patterns of thoughts, behaviors, and beliefs ingrained within us through our upbringing, culture, society, and past experiences. These conditioned patterns of energy often shape our perceptions of ourselves, others, and the world around us.

To delve deeper into this concept, envision a web of energies and frequencies interwoven to form the fabric of your essence. Each thread represents a distinct experience, intertwining to shape the unique patterns of your being. From moments of joy to trials of adversity, every encounter leaves an indelible mark, contributing to the rich tapestry of your soul.

Every day, as vibrant, energetic beings, we naturally interact with these energies and frequencies, both internal and external. We resonate with certain ones based on our inner state and the vibrations of the external world. This interaction can either uplift us, aligning us with higher states of consciousness and well-being, or hinder our growth, perpetuating patterns of limitation and suffering. Through cultivating awareness and mindfulness, we can become more attuned to these energetic dynamics. We can discern which energies are serving our highest good and which are holding us back. Practices such as meditation, self-reflection, and conscious intention-setting empower us to align ourselves with energies that support our growth, healing, and evolution.

Ultimately, recognizing ourselves as beings of energy allows us to approach life with greater sensitivity, authenticity, and empowerment. We become active participants in the co-creation of our reality, harnessing the power of energy to manifest our deepest desires and fulfill our highest potential.

The Ego and the Observer

Do you ever feel like your mind is playing a relentless game of tug-of-war with your emotions? One moment you're sailing smoothly through life, and the next, you're caught in a whirlwind of triggers, anxieties, and doubts. Welcome to the fascinating labyrinth of the human mind, where the intricate dance between thoughts and emotions can leave us feeling like mere spectators of our own lives.

Imagine your mind as a bustling marketplace, filled with vendors hawking their wares of thoughts, beliefs, and perceptions. At the heart of this bustling bazaar stands the ego, the grand orchestrator of it all. The ego is like the narrator of our life story, constantly weaving tales about who we are, what we should fear, and how we should react.

For instance, consider a scenario where you receive constructive criticism at work. Your mind, under the influence of the ego, might interpret this feedback as a personal attack on your competence. Suddenly, you find

Iris Awakens to Her Path

In the quiet moments of early mornings, I would sit beside my grandfather, absorbing the cadence of prayers that danced from his lips—a ritual as familiar as the sunrise. One day, curiosity bubbled within me, and I dared to ask him about the words that wove a tapestry of gratitude each day.

In response, he unveiled a revelation that sprang from the depths of tradition. At the tender age of six, I struggled to fathom why he thanked God for not being born a girl. Perplexed, I questioned him, unaware of the ancient layers beneath his words. His answer seemed paradoxical; he spoke of blessings bestowed upon girls, a sentiment that clashed with my innocent understanding.

For years, the truth remained shrouded, concealed beneath theprotective embrace of my grandfather—a guardian shielding his grandchild from the harsh realities of life. The origins of his dailygratitude unfolded as a poignant acknowledgment of the perils women face during childbirth. In the canvas of my young mind, a dissonance persisted, a puzzle piece yearning to slot into its rightful place.

In the sacred space of the synagogue, a subtle divide revealed itself. My brother, by virtue of his gender, could touch the Torah, while an invisible barrier restrained me. A disconcerting awareness settled in—a contradiction between the messages of equality and capability instilled by my parents and the limitations imposed within those hallowed walls.

This dissonance echoed through my experiences, creating a sense of being held within the confines of my gender. In the eyes of tradition, a distinction persisted, leaving me to grapple with the incongruities of a world that proclaimed equality yet adhered to age-old norms.

As an adult, I delved deeper into the labyrinth of incongruence within myself, tracing the origins of my triggers. It's a journey that took me back to my formative years, where I unwittingly absorbed the expectations of those around me like a sponge. Growing up, I envisioned my life unfolding much like the glamorous tales portrayed in movies—a trajectory that seemed predetermined. I began to question the source of these expectations. Whose ideal life was I striving for? It became evident that the glossy images I chased weren't my own aspirations, but rather the collective dreams of my tribe. This realization set me on a roller coaster of emotions—the thrill of achieving societal milestones followed by the crushing disappointment when the euphoria faded, leaving me adrift in a sea of discontent. The journey of understanding had just begun, and the whispers of disparity lingered within the sacred spaces of my upbringing.

My tribe had ingrained in me the belief that struggle was the price of admission to a life of joy, happiness, and freedom. I internalized the notion that success required sacrifice—a piece of my soul offered up in exchange for the fleeting moments of ecstasy I glimpsed on the silver screen. But as I embarked on the journey of self-discovery, I realized that true liberation lay in dismantling these deeply entrenched beliefs. I began to question the validity of the narratives I'd been fed and to challenge the assumption that happiness could only be found through struggle and sacrifice.

In unraveling the origins of the incongruence I had felt for so long, I uncovered a profound truth: each of us holds the power to redefine our own narrative. We can forge a path that resonates with our authentic self, free from the shackles of societal expectations. It was a revelation that sparked a sense of empowerment—a recognition that true joy and fulfillment could only be found by embracing my individuality and living life on my own terms.

yourself spiraling into self-doubt and defensiveness. This reaction is entirely orchestrated by the persuasive whispers of the ego.

What makes the ego such a formidable force is our innate tendency to believe its every proclamation. We're wired to trust our thoughts and perceptions implicitly, even when they lead us down the rabbit hole of negativity and self-sabotage. It's as if we've handed over the keys to our happiness and well-being to a cunning trickster disguised as our own mind.

Consider the common belief: "I'm not good enough." This insidious thought can worm its way into the fabric of our consciousness, dictating our actions and coloring our perceptions of ourselves and the world around us. Before we know it, we're trapped in a self-fulfilling prophecy, all because we bought into the mind's persuasive rhetoric.

But here's the secret to reclaiming your power: become the observer of your own mind. Instead of being swept away by the ceaseless chatter of thoughts and emotions, as you react to your triggers, imagine yourself stepping back and watching the spectacle unfold with a sense of detached curiosity. You can learn to unravel the thoughts and beliefs that hold you back and, instead, reclaim ownership of your mind. Let's explore how the mind and the ego are intertwined, how the ego obstructs the mind's clarity, and most importantly, how you can break free from its grasp.

Imagine you're walking down a crowded street, lost in thought. Suddenly, a passerby bumps into you, and you feel a surge of anger rising within you. But is it truly your anger, or is it a projection of the ego's insecurities causing you to react as if the person intentionally jostled you to show how insignificant you are? Our minds often fall victim to the ego's tricks. Your ego convinces you that every thought, every emotion, is a reflection of your true self. Yet, in truth these rise to the surface through a sea of conditioning, biases, and fears—manifestations of the ego's influence.

At times we feel plagued by a relentless barrage of negative thoughts. This is the ego at work, constructing barriers that inhibit our mind's natural flow. It convinces us that we are in control while steering us away from the truth—that our mind's thoughts are not necessarily our own truth. Using this illusion of self-control, the ego blinds us to our limitless potential within.

Recognizing and being aware of the ego's deception is the first step towards reclaiming control of our minds and minimizing the ego's presence and influence on our thoughts and actions. By cultivating mindfulness and embracing self-compassion, we can dismantle the barriers erected by the ego and reconnect with our authentic selves. Remember, you are not defined by your thoughts; you are the observer, the witness to the ever-changing landscape of the mind. By learning to observe your mind with compassion and awareness, you can break free from your old narrative patterns and write the script of your own life.

When you become the observer of your behavior, you gain insight into the patterns and tendencies that drive you and result in repetitive, undesired outcomes. The moment you start questioning why you continuously encounter the same themes in your life—whether it's consistently dating similar types of people, facing recurrent job terminations, engaging in constant power struggles, succumbing to unhealthy eating habits, procrastinating, repeating self-sabotaging behaviors, or any behavior you ultimately would like to stop engaging in—signifies a profound shift in perspective. It marks your initial transition into the role of an observer. Instead of being ensnared in the repetitive loop of events, you've chosen to step back and evaluate the situation from a more detached viewpoint.

When we learn to observe the motivations behind our actions, as well as the consequences they produce, we are able to see ourselves more objectively, free from the biases and narratives that often cloud our perception. We become the observer of our own behavior when we step back from actively participating in our actions and instead observe them from a detached standpoint. Cultivating a sense of mindfulness and self-awareness allows us to witness our thoughts, emotions, and actions without judgment or attachment.

Becoming an observer requires a heightened level of consciousness, and through this process, we gain a deeper understanding of our internal landscape and the patterns that shape our experiences. By questioning why certain themes persist, we begin to recognize the underlying factors influencing our circumstances. We can better understand the impact of our behavior on ourselves and others, and we can identify areas for growth and change, as well as recognize moments when we may be acting out of alignment with our values or intentions. This newfound awareness sets the stage for personal growth and transformation as we strive to break free from limiting patterns and create a more fulfilling life. Ultimately, being the observer empowers us to make conscious choices and experience a greater sense of agency in our lives.

Once you acknowledge these patterns, the next step is to accept them without judgment, understanding their origins and underlying causes, and cultivating mindfulness to observe your thoughts and emotions without being overwhelmed by them. The practice of observing the mind and its incessant chatter creates a sense of separation and disassociation from the commentary. As we step back from engaging with these thoughts, we discover a silent, unchanging awareness behind them, merely observing without attachment. Self-compassion plays a crucial role in this process, encouraging you to treat yourself with kindness and understanding as you navigate triggers and old patterns. Reframing your perspective can help you view triggers as opportunities for growth rather than obstacles, fostering a sense of empowerment.

Triggers persistently resurface for a reason, imprinting similar patterns across our experiences. These echoes serve as guides, revealing the underlying themes of our consciousness. Wherever we venture, our inner struggles follow like a shadow, urging us to confront and transcend them. Our reactions to these triggers, not the external factors themselves, dictate much of our life's challenges. Our sense of fulfillment and distress hinges on our state of consciousness, a realm we can always nurture, evolve, and expand.

What I Am...

What I Am Meant to Know, Remember, Learn

Inherent in our existence is our drive to decipher the enigma of our existence. Beyond the confines of our physicality lies a realm of consciousness, where the essence of our being resides. We are not merely products of flesh and bone but vessels teeming with the potential for profound enlightenment and evolution. Your journey of self-discovery is an odyssey that transcends the mundane and delves into the depths of your innermost self. Fueled by an insatiable thirst for understanding and a relentless pursuit of truth, you will encounter myriad revelations and epiphanies that illuminate your path.

At the core of this exploration lies the fundamental question of identity—who are we and what is our purpose in this vast universe? Through introspective contemplation, we begin to unravel the layers of conditioning and societal constructs that veil our true essence. In this process, we unearth the truths that resonate with our souls and align with the divine blueprint of our existence.

The journey of self-discovery is not without its challenges and obstacles. Along the way, we confront our deepest fears, insecurities, and limitations, transcending them with courage and resilience. Each trial we encounter serves as a crucible for transformation, forging us into beings of greater wisdom, compassion, and authenticity. Guiding us through this labyrinth of existence is our innate knowing—a quiet voice that whispers truths beyond the realm of words. This intuitive wisdom tells us how to uncover the mysteries of our being and discern the path that leads to fulfillment and enlightenment. Ultimately, the journey of self-discovery is a sacred pilgrimage—a quest for the soul's reunion with its source. In the labyrinth of existence, we are not merely wanderers but seekers of truth, destined to unveil the divine mysteries that lie within and without.

In our exploration of the essence of self, we embark on a profound journey inward, peeling away the layers that shroud our true nature. As we delve into the depths of our being, we encounter a myriad of identities—the roles we play, the labels we adopt, the expectations imposed upon us by society. Yet, beneath this veneer lies something more profound, something eternal and immutable.

At the very core of our existence, we find the essence of love. It is the primal force that animates our being, the sacred energy that binds us to one another and to the universe at large. Love is not merely an emotion or a fleeting sentiment; it is the very fabric of our reality, the essence of who we truly are.

Through introspection and reflection, we can experience the realization that our essence transcends the limitations of our ego, extending far beyond the confines of our individuality. Love is the essence of our true nature, the source from which all of creation emanates. It is the unconditional acceptance of ourselves and others, the recognition of our interconnectedness and unity with all of existence.

As we continue to explore the essence of self, we uncover the beauty of our unique expression of love. We recognize that love is not something that we must seek outside of ourselves but something that we carry within us, always and forever. It is the guiding light that illuminates our path, the source of strength and resilience in the face of adversity.

In embracing our true essence as love, we liberate ourselves from the shackles of ego and embrace the fullness of our being. We recognize that love is not something that we must earn or strive for but something that flows effortlessly from the depths of our being. And in doing so, we awaken to the boundless potential that resides within us, ready to be expressed in its fullest, most authentic form.

In the vast tapestry of existence, our true purpose emerges as an expression of love. As we navigate the complexities of life, it is easy to lose sight of this fundamental truth. Yet, our journey of self-discovery is one of remembrance that rekindles the flame of love that resides within us and illuminates our path.

At the heart of our purpose lies a profound calling to embody love in all its forms. Love is not merely an emotion but a force of transformation, a catalyst for healing and growth. Through contemplation and soul-searching, we reconnect with the essence of love that permeates every aspect of our being.

In remembering our purpose, we come to understand that we are here to cultivate love in ourselves and in the world around us. This may manifest in various ways—through acts of kindness and compassion, through creative expression and service to others. Whatever form it takes, our purpose is to be a vessel of love, radiating its light into the darkest corners of existence.

As we uncover the passions and talents that align with our higher calling, we find fulfillment and meaning in the pursuit of love. We realize that our purpose is not something external to be attained but something inherent within us, waiting to be expressed. It is the recognition that we are intrinsically connected to all of creation, and that our actions have the power to ripple outwards, touching the lives of others in profound and meaningful ways.

In embracing love as our purpose, we step into our true power and potential. We become agents of change, catalysts for transformation, and beacons of light in a world that often feels dark and divided. And in doing so, we fulfill our deepest longing—to be vessels of love in a world that so desperately needs it.

Embracing Love's Wisdom Within

In the depths of our being lies a reservoir of wisdom, intricately intertwined with the essence of love. At the core of our being, love serves as both the source and the conduit of wisdom. It is through love that we cultivate an intimate connection with the innate intelligence of the universe, tapping into the boundless wisdom that flows through all of creation. In this exploration, we come to understand that love is not only the destination but also the journey itself, guiding us towards deeper insights and greater understanding.

Through mindfulness practices and inner reflection, we learn to quiet the noise of the external world and listen to the whispers of our intuition. Love gently nudges us towards alignment with our true purpose and highest potential, offering guidance and support every step of the way. As we cultivate a sense of presence and awareness, we become attuned to the subtle nuances of our inner landscape, recognizing the wisdom that lies dormant within us, waiting to be unleashed.

Trusting in the wisdom of love, we surrender to the flow of life and embrace the path that unfolds before us. We relinquish the need for control and allow ourselves to be guided by the currents of divine intelligence. In doing so, we find solace in the knowledge that we are held and supported by a force greater than ourselves, a force that is rooted in love and compassion.

Wisdom is not something to be acquired or attained but a gift that resides within us, waiting to be discovered. Love serves as the key that unlocks this treasure trove of knowledge, inviting us to embrace the fullness of our being and live our lives in alignment with our deepest truth. Through love's wisdom, we navigate the complexities of existence with grace and ease, knowing that we are always guided by the infinite intelligence of the universe.

Love's Path to Growth & Transformation

In the grand tapestry of life, love serves as the guiding force propelling us towards growth and transformation. It invites us to embrace the journey of evolution with open arms, recognizing that love is both the catalyst and the destination of our personal growth.

Life, as we know it, is a continuous cycle of change and adaptation. Through the lens of love, we perceive every challenge and obstacle as an opportunity for growth. Love teaches us to embrace change with grace and resilience, knowing that each experience is a stepping stone on our path towards self-realization. As we confront the challenges that stand in the way of our personal growth, love provides us with the courage and strength to persevere. It is through the lens of love that we are able to navigate the uncertainties of life with an open heart and a steadfast resolve.

Love encourages us to step outside of our comfort zones and explore new horizons. When we face adversity, we discover our true potential and unlock new levels of understanding and self-awareness. Love teaches us to embrace vulnerability as a gateway to transformation, allowing us to shed the layers of conditioning and fear that inhibit our growth.

In the journey of growth and transformation, love serves as our constant companion, guiding us towards our highest potential. Through the lens of love we are able to cultivate a sense of compassion and empathy towards ourselves and others, fostering deeper connections and nurturing our collective evolution.

As we embrace the path of growth and transformation with love as our guide, we awaken to the infinite possibilities that lie before us. Love reminds us that we are not defined by our past or limited by our circumstances, but rather empowered to create the reality we desire. Through the transformative power of love, we emerge as the architects of our destiny, propelled towards a future filled with boundless potential and endless possibilities.

In the journey of understanding triggers, we confront a profound truth: transformation is an inside job. Viewed through a spiritual lens, this insight transcends the realm of mere understanding; it becomes a guiding principle, illuminating our path towards growth and enlightenment. Rather than seeking external fixes or attributing our experiences solely to outside forces, we're called to turn inward, recognizing the inherent power and potential within ourselves to effect profound change.

Within the realm of spirituality, the concept of "transforming from the inside out" is not merely theoretical but deeply experiential. It's about engaging with our triggers as invitations to explore the inner landscape—the terrain of our thoughts, emotions, beliefs, and subconscious patterns. By courageously delving into these inner realms, we begin to recognize the intricate interplay between our inner world and outer experiences. Triggers, once perceived as external disruptions, are reframed as sacred messengers, guiding us towards greater self-awareness and spiritual awakening. Through the lens of inner transformation, we come to understand that our external reality is but a reflection of our internal state—a mirror reflecting back the aspects of ourselves in need of healing, integration, or release. If we harbor negative thoughts, emotions, or limiting beliefs, we are likely to attract similar experiences into our lives. Conversely, when we cultivate positive thoughts, emotions, and beliefs, our external reality tends to reflect this inner harmony and positivity.

Moreover, the process of transforming from the inside out profoundly influences our response to triggers. Instead of reacting from a place of unconsciousness or conditioned patterns, we cultivate a mindful awareness, observing our thoughts and emotions with compassion and curiosity. This shift in perspective empowers us to transcend habitual reactions and choose conscious responses aligned with our highest truth and purpose.

Ultimately, the journey of inner transformation is a sacred pilgrimage—a quest for self-realization and spiritual liberation. It's a journey of reclaiming our inherent divinity and embodying the fullness of our authentic selves. By embracing the spiritual perspective of transformation, we embark on a path towards greater self-awareness, inner peace, and spiritual fulfillment. Through the alchemy of inner work, we move beyond the limitations of the egoic mind, awakening to the boundless depths of our being and the infinite possibilities that await us on the journey ahead.

The essence of inner transformation is deeply rooted in the core teachings of spirituality. It begins with the recognition that our external experiences are intricately intertwined with our internal landscape. This profound insight suggests that the quality of our thoughts, emotions, beliefs, and consciousness shapes the reality we perceive and experience. This understanding underscores the importance of turning our focus inward when seeking transformation. Rather than searching for solutions or validation outside of ourselves, we are encouraged to embark on a journey of self-exploration and introspection. By delving into the depths of our being with openness and curiosity, we uncover the root causes of our challenges and triggers.

This process of inner exploration allows us to identify and address patterns of thought, emotion, and behavior that no longer serve our highest good. It involves shining the light of awareness into the shadowy corners of our psyche, confronting our fears, insecurities, and unresolved traumas with courage and compassion.

As we navigate this inner terrain, we may encounter resistance and discomfort. Yet, it is through this process of facing our inner demons that we facilitate profound healing and transformation. By acknowledging and integrating the aspects of ourselves that we have suppressed or denied, we reclaim our wholeness and authenticity.

Moreover, as we undergo inner transformation, we begin to notice shifts in our external reality. As our thoughts become more positive and aligned with our highest truth, we attract experiences and opportunities that reflect this newfound inner harmony. Relationships become more fulfilling, circumstances align in our favor, and we experience a greater sense of peace and fulfillment in our lives.

Ultimately, the essence of inner transformation lies in the recognition that we possess the power to shape our reality from the inside out. By cultivating self-awareness, mindfulness, and a deep connection to our inner wisdom, we unlock the door to profound personal growth and spiritual evolution. As we embrace this journey of self-discovery and inner exploration, we awaken to the limitless potential that resides within us, and we step into our true power as creators of our own reality.

Understanding triggers within the context of inner transformation is essential for navigating the intricate landscape of personal growth and spiritual evolution. Triggers, whether they manifest as subtle nuances or blatant provocations, act as powerful messengers guiding us towards deeper self-awareness and healing.

Rather than perceiving triggers as mere inconveniences or challenges to overcome, we can choose to embrace them as sacred invitations for inner exploration. Each trigger serves as a mirror, reflecting back to us aspects of ourselves that may be buried beneath the surface of our consciousness. These reflections offer invaluable insights into our innermost thoughts, emotions, beliefs, and patterns of behavior.

When we encounter a trigger, it's an opportunity to pause and inquire within. What is it about this situation or circumstance that evokes such a strong emotional response within me? What underlying beliefs or past experiences are being activated? By quieting our ego and delving into these questions with honesty and curiosity, we begin to unravel the layers of our psyche, gaining deeper insight into our inner landscape.

Moreover, examining our triggers provides us with the opportunity to engage in the process of healing, integration, and release. As we shine the light of awareness onto the wounds and traumas that lie beneath our triggered reactions, we create space for healing to occur. Through practices such as mindfulness, self-reflection, and compassionate inquiry, we can begin to cultivate a sense of inner peace and wholeness while casting aside the limitations of our past experiences.

Healing our triggers offers us the chance to integrate fragmented aspects of ourselves that have been disowned or denied. Often, our triggered reactions stem from unresolved issues or unmet needs that have been buried deep within our subconscious. By acknowledging and embracing these parts of ourselves with love and acceptance, we can reintegrate them into our conscious awareness, reclaiming our power and authenticity in the process.

Ultimately, understanding triggers within the context of inner transformation empowers us to take on life's challenges with grace and resilience. Instead of being at the mercy of our triggered reactions, we can cultivate a sense of inner peace and equanimity, knowing that each trigger serves as a steppingstone on the path to greater self-awareness and spiritual awakening. As we adopt this perspective, we unlock the door to profound personal growth and transformation, paving the way for a life of greater joy, fulfillment, and authenticity.

Inner Alchemy

The process of inner alchemy represents a sacred journey of self-transformation and spiritual evolution. Drawing from ancient wisdom traditions and modern practices alike, this transformative process invites us to embark on a profound exploration of our inner landscape. At the heart of inner alchemy lies the recognition that our consciousness is the alchemical laboratory in which profound transformation occurs. Through various spiritual practices and modalities, we engage in the sacred work of transmuting our inner lead—our conditioned patterns, limiting beliefs, and unresolved emotions—into spiritual gold—our innate wisdom, compassion, and authenticity.

One of the fundamental practices of inner alchemy is mindfulness meditation. By cultivating present-moment awareness and observing the contents of our mind without judgment, we gain insight into the subtle workings of our inner world. Through mindfulness, we become adept at recognizing the habitual thought patterns and emotional reactions that often drive our behavior, allowing us to consciously choose how we respond to the triggers and challenges of life.

Contemplative prayer is another potent tool in the alchemical toolkit. Through prayer, we open our hearts to the divine presence within and without, surrendering our egoic desires and attachments to a higher power. In this state of surrender, we cultivate a deep sense of trust and faith in the unfolding of life, allowing divine wisdom to guide our actions and decisions.

Yogic philosophy and practices offer yet another avenue for inner alchemy. Through the practices of asana (physical postures), pranayama (breathwork), and meditation, we harmonize the body, mind, and spirit, creating a conducive environment for spiritual growth and transformation. By aligning ourselves with the principles of yoga—such as non-violence, truthfulness, and self-discipline—we purify our consciousness and awaken to our true nature as divine beings.

Shamanic journeying provides a yet another approach to inner alchemy, tapping into the wisdom of indigenous traditions and the spirit world. Through guided journeys and rituals, we traverse the realms of the unconscious, encountering spirit guides, power animals, and ancestral wisdom. In these sacred journeys, we gain insight into the deeper layers of our psyche, uncovering hidden truths and accessing the healing energies of the unseen realms.

Regardless of the specific practices we choose to engage in, the essence of inner alchemy remains the same: the conscious, intentional exploration and transformation of our inner landscape. As we embark on this sacred journey, we gradually unravel the layers of conditioning, egoic patterns, and unconscious biases that veil our true essence. Through dedication, self-inquiry, and surrender, we emerge from the alchemical crucible transformed—awakening to the radiant truth of our being and embodying the fullness of our divine potential.

Embracing the Shadow

Central to the journey of inner transformation is the courageous exploration of our shadow—the often overlooked or denied aspects of ourselves that dwell in the depths of our psyche. These shadow elements represent the parts of us that we have deemed undesirable, stemming from experiences of shame, fear, or trauma. Yet, when we face and integrate these aspects into our sense of self, we unlock profound opportunities for growth and healing.

The shadow encompasses a myriad of emotions, desires, and behaviors that we have pushed into the darkness of our subconscious mind. These may include feelings of anger, jealousy, insecurity, or unworthiness, as well as aspects of our personality that we have deemed socially unacceptable. By denying these aspects of ourselves, we inadvertently give them power over us, fueling unconscious patterns and triggers that influence our thoughts, emotions, and actions.

To embark on the journey of inner transformation is to bravely shine the light of awareness into the depths of our shadow, acknowledging and embracing all facets of our being with unconditional love and acceptance. It is a process of reclaiming and integrating these disowned parts, recognizing that they too hold valuable lessons and wisdom for our growth and evolution.

In facing our shadow, we may encounter resistance, discomfort, or even fear. Yet, through this courageous exploration we begin to unravel the layers of conditioning and unconscious patterns that have bound us to self-limitation and suffering. As we shine the light of awareness onto our shadow, we begin to transform fear into acceptance, shame into compassion, and judgment into understanding. By embracing all aspects of ourselves with love and acceptance, we reclaim our power and authenticity, stepping into the fullness of who we truly are.

The Awakening of Consciousness

As we delve further into the realms of inner transformation, we undergo a profound awakening to the inherent wisdom and divinity that lie dormant within us. This awakening is marked by moments of insight, revelation, and spiritual epiphany, where the veils of illusion are lifted, and we perceive the world with newfound clarity and depth.

Through this awakening, we transcend the limitations of the egoic mind and the illusion of separation, recognizing the interconnectedness of all life. We come to understand that we are not isolated beings, but rather interconnected expressions of the universal source of love and light. In this realization, we experience a profound sense of unity and oneness with all that exists.

With each step on this sacred journey, our consciousness expands, allowing us to perceive reality from a higher perspective. We begin to see beyond the surface level of appearances and tap into the underlying truths that govern existence. We recognize the inherent divinity within ourselves and all beings, and we embrace the interconnected web of life with reverence and gratitude.

This awakening of consciousness is not merely intellectual or conceptual but deeply experiential. This shift in perception penetrates to the core of our being, transforming how we relate to ourselves, others, and the world around us. We no longer see ourselves as separate entities struggling to survive in a hostile world, but instead we recognize we are an integral part of a greater whole, each playing a unique role in the cosmic dance of creation.

In this awakened state, we are able to navigate the ups and downs of life with grace and equanimity. We no longer cling to the transient pleasures and pains of the material world but instead find solace in the eternal truths that lie beyond the realm of form. We cultivate a sense of inner peace and contentment that transcends the fluctuations of external circumstances, knowing that our true nature is timeless and boundless.

Ultimately, the awakening of consciousness is the culmination of the journey of inner transformation. It is a return to our true essence—a recognition of the divine spark that resides within us and all of creation. As we embrace this awakened state, we become vessels of love and light, shining forth our authentic selves, and contributing to the collective evolution of consciousness.

"We are transforming from the inside out" serves as more than a mere statement; it embodies a profound invitation to embark on the greatest adventure of all: the journey of self-discovery and spiritual awakening. This journey, rooted in the process of inner transformation, calls on you to reclaim your inherent wholeness and rediscover the boundless depths of your being.

In the face of triggers and challenges, remember that the greatest catalysts for growth lie within you. They are not obstacles to be avoided or feared but sacred opportunities for self-awareness and evolution. By embracing the process of inner transformation with courage and compassion, you can unlock the doors to profound personal growth and spiritual awakening. As you journey inward, approach each trigger with openness and curiosity, knowing that they hold the keys to your deepest healing and liberation. Shine the light of awareness into the shadowy corners of your psyche, embracing all aspects of your various selves with love and acceptance.

In this journey of self-discovery, remember that you are not alone. You are supported by the wisdom of the ages and the collective consciousness of all beings. Together, let us embark on this sacred quest, knowing that the destination is not a place but a state of being—an ever-deepening realization of our true nature as expressions of love and light.

As you navigate the twists and turns of this inner journey, may you find solace in the knowledge that you are forever evolving, forever expanding, forever becoming more fully yourself. And in the end, may you emerge from the depths of your being, radiant and whole, ready to embrace the beauty and wonder of life in all its myriad forms.

Chapter 5

Change Versus Transformation

In the preceding chapter, we delved into the profound notion of transformation and its significance in our lives. We discussed the concept of transforming from the inside out, emphasizing the fundamental disparity between surface-level change and the enduring metamorphosis of the soul. While change may alter our circumstances and behaviors temporarily, true transformation transcends superficial modifications, reaching deep into the essence of our being. Now let's explore what authentic transformation is, what its process and manifestations look like, and how to distinguish it from mere change. We will illuminate the profound impact it can have on our lives.

Change is a constant on the path of human existence. It manifests in various forms, from shifting circumstances to altering perspectives. However, change often operates on the surface level, addressing external manifestations without penetrating the core of our being. It is akin to rearranging the furniture in a room without addressing the shortcomings of the underlying architecture. While such changes may offer temporary reprieve or novelty, they fail to evoke lasting fulfillment or growth.

In contrast, transformation operates at a deeper, more profound level. It entails a fundamental shift in consciousness, values, and beliefs, leading to a metamorphosis of the soul. Unlike change, which is often driven by external stimuli or circumstances, transformation emanates from within, originating in the depths of our being. It is not merely about adapting to new circumstances but about evolving into a higher state of being, transcending our limitations, and realizing our true potential.

True transformation is a multifaceted passage, encompassing various stages and dimensions. At its core lies self-awareness, the foundation upon which the structure of transformation is built. Self-awareness requires honest introspection, a willingness to confront our fears, limitations, and shadow aspects. It is through this process of self-examination that we lay bare the layers of conditioning and societal programming that have veiled our authentic selves.

From self-awareness springs acceptance, the acknowledgment and embracing of all facets of our being, both light and shadow. Acceptance is not resignation but empowerment, for it liberates us from the shackles of judgment, shame, and self-criticism, allowing us to appreciate our inherent worthiness and potential for growth.

Accompanying acceptance is surrender, the relinquishment of control and the ego's incessant striving. In surrender, we open ourselves to the wisdom of the universe, trusting in the inherent intelligence of life to guide us on our journey. It is through surrender we transcend the limited perspective of the ego and align ourselves with the greater flow of existence.

From surrender emerges integration, the harmonization of disparate aspects of ourselves into a cohesive whole. When we acknowledge our contradictions and paradoxes and recognize that our perceived flaws are integral to our wholeness, we experience a marriage of selves. It is through this integration that we reclaim disowned aspects of ourselves and embody our true authenticity.

Integration is the process of accepting the dormant facets of our being we have long disowned or neglected. When we confront and embrace these suppressed parts of ourselves, we move towards wholeness and authenticity. Through integration, we acknowledge the complexity of our identity, accepting both the light and shadow aspects that shape who we are. By reclaiming these disowned elements, we not only gain a deeper

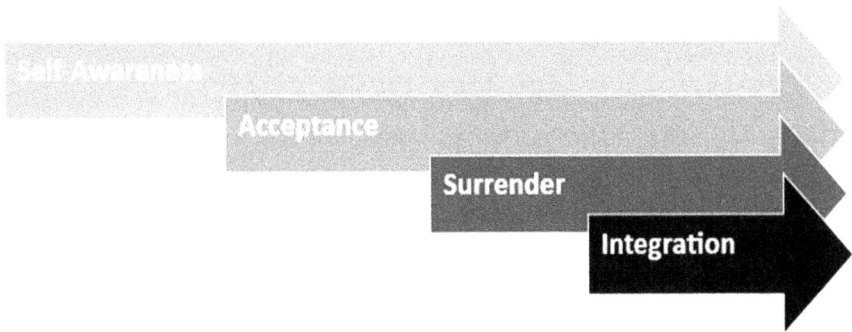

understanding of ourselves but also cultivate a sense of inner harmony and balance. This process allows us to move beyond the limitations of societal conditioning or past traumas, empowering us to live more fully and authentically.

Embodying our true authenticity requires a willingness to delve into the depths of our psyche and confront the aspects of ourselves that we may have shunned or denied. Integration invites us to accept our contradictions, recognizing that our flaws and imperfections are integral parts of our humanity. As we integrate these disparate components of our identity, we no longer feel fragmented or at odds with ourselves. Instead, we become more aligned with our core values and beliefs, living in alignment with our true essence. Through integration, we not only honor our individuality but also contribute to the collective of the human experience, embodying authenticity in its purest form. Integration is an important step on the path of transformation.

Transformational Manifestations

The manifestations of true transformation are manifold, permeating every aspect of our lives. On the external level, transformation may manifest as changes in behavior, habits, and relationships. However, these outward manifestations are merely the tip of the iceberg, reflecting the deeper shifts occurring within.

At the emotional level, transformation may manifest as a newfound sense of peace, joy, and fulfillment. As we release the burdens of the past and embrace the present moment, we experience a profound sense of lightness and aliveness. Emotions once suppressed or denied may flow freely, enriching our experience of life and deepening our connection to others.

On the mental level, transformation may manifest as clarity, insight, and wisdom. As we transcend the limitations of conditioned thinking and egoic identification, we gain access to a higher perspective, free from the distortions of fear and judgment. Our minds become clear and luminous, capable of discerning truth amidst the myriad illusions of the world.

At the spiritual level, transformation may manifest as a deepening connection to the divine or the sacred essence of life. As we transcend the boundaries of the ego and merge with the infinite source of being, we experience a profound sense of oneness and unity with all creation. Spirituality ceases to be a mere belief system or ideology and instead becomes a lived experience, infusing every moment with a sense of reverence and awe.

True transformation is not merely about changing our circumstances or behaviors but about undergoing a profound metamorphosis of the soul. Transformation's journey of self-discovery, acceptance, surrender, and integration, culminates in a deeper alignment with our authentic selves and the larger tapestry of existence. While change may offer temporary relief or novelty, true transformation brings about lasting fulfillment, joy, and meaning. As we embark on this sacred path of self-realization, may we learn to value the inherent beauty and potential within ourselves and cultivate a life of purpose, passion, and profound inner peace. The Process can be an integral part of your transformation by the releasing of triggers and layers blocking your path.

The Power of The Process

As we release triggers and barriers that impede our path, we free up our energy and carve out room for growth. Whether we're conscious of it or not, we are in a perpetual dialogue with the universe, that ethereal domain of energy. Through this process of expanding our energy, we are not only opening up new dimensions within ourselves but also making way for experiences that diverge from our past encounters.

Consider this realm that exists beyond the tangible, a realm woven with the threads of energy that bind us all. In this ethereal realm, the dance of life unfolds in synchronicity with our thoughts, emotions, and intentions. When we consciously engage with this energetic realm, we wield the power to shape our reality in ways that transcend the limitations of the physical world. One such profound act is the creation of energetic space—a process that removes our triggers and blocks, allowing our energy to expand and inviting the universe to bestow upon us its everyday miracles.

Picture a cluttered room—a space filled to the brim with belongings accumulated over the years. Each item carries its own energetic imprint, occupying valuable space and hindering the flow of energy within the room. Similarly, our minds and spirits can become cluttered with triggers and blocks—negative thoughts, past traumas, limiting beliefs—that constrict our energy and impede our ability to manifest our desires.

Removing these triggers and blocks is akin to decluttering the room of our psyche, creating spaciousness for energy to flow freely. As we release the grip of fear, doubt, and resentment, we feel a sense of lightness permeate our being—a weight lifted, a burden eased. In this state of expanded energy, we become like magnets, effortlessly drawing towards us the blessings and miracles that enrich our lives.

The universe, it seems, speaks in the language of energy—a language understood not by the ears but by the heart and soul. When we clear away the debris of negativity and resistance, we send a powerful message to the cosmos—we are ready to receive. It is as though we have opened wide the doors of our being, inviting the universe to shower us with its boundless abundance.

And so, the everyday miracles begin to unfold, like delicate flower petals unfurling in the morning sun. Perhaps it is the serendipitous alignment of traffic lights, granting us a smooth drive to our destination. Or maybe it is the sudden appearance of an unexpected windfall—a sale that makes the dress we have been eyeing affordable, a generous gift from a friend, or a lucrative opportunity that falls into our lap.

Miracles need not always be grand or extravagant to be profound. Sometimes, they manifest in the simplest of gestures—a warm smile from a stranger, a kind word from a colleague, or the embrace of a loved one. Even our normally aloof teenager offering us an authentic hug can be a testament to the magic that infuses our lives when we open ourselves to receive.

In creating energetic space, we enter into a state of co-creation with the universe—a dance of give and take, of surrender and receptivity. We release the need to control and manipulate outcomes, trusting instead in the inherent benevolence of the cosmos. In doing so, we align ourselves with the natural rhythms of life, allowing abundance to flow effortlessly into our experience.

It is said that miracles are not contrary to nature but only contrary to what we know about nature. When we expand our perception of reality to encompass the unseen realms of energy and consciousness, we open ourselves to a world of infinite possibilities. And in this wondrous realm, miracles abound, waiting patiently for us to claim them as our own.

Dear seeker of miracles, we invite you to take a moment to breathe deeply and feel into the expansiveness of your being. Release the grip of resistance and allow your energy to flow freely, unencumbered by the burdens of the past. Know that as you create space within yourself, you create space for the universe to work its magic in your life. Embrace the journey with an open heart and a spirit of gratitude and watch in awe as the everyday miracles unfold before your eyes.

By actively participating in The Process, you embark on a path to uncover and dismantle the barriers that hinder your connection with the unseen dimensions of existence. This transformative endeavor is not intended as a one-time solution but rather as a continual practice ingrained in your daily life. Its straightforward nature enables you to integrate it seamlessly into your routine, serving as a reliable tool in your arsenal for cultivating authenticity. By incorporating it into your habits, you enhance your ability to discern moments when your actions deviate from your true self, thus progressing along the path towards self-realization.

Understandably, you may be saying to yourself right now, "That sounds nice, but my life is such a mess, it feels impossible." This is a relatable sentiment that may be steeped in a mixture of guilt, shame, and anger over past missteps or perceived failures, emotions that have a remarkable knack for chaining us to a history we cannot change. And yet, equally futile is the worry over a future yet to unfold, for no amount of fretting alters its eventual outcome.

Yes, there is wisdom in planning for the future, in setting goals and aspirations. But amidst the meticulous crafting of tomorrow's dreams, we shouldn't ignore the profound power of being fully in the present moment. It is here, in the now, where we can tap into the boundless energy of God and the universe, recognizing that this immense power is not some distant force but an intrinsic part of our being.

Yet, we've been conditioned to doubt ourselves, to believe that we are somehow unworthy or inadequate to wield such power. But in truth, there's no prerequisite of being "good enough." Rooting our everyday choices in love rather than fear, judgment, or shame will arm you with that power. With each loving choice, we inch closer to alignment with the infinite strength that resides within us.

Confronting our inner selves and our programming can be scary and daunting. But as we step away from fear and towards love, we create the space for everyday miracles to unfurl before us. Miracles need not be grandiose; they can manifest in the quiet moments of connection, the subtle shifts of perspective, or the gentle healing of old wounds.

And if, in moments of doubt, faith feels elusive, there are beacons to guide us. We can lean on the faith of those who have walked this path before us, those who have witnessed firsthand the transformative power of choosing love over fear. Their faith becomes a lifeline, a reminder that within each of us lies the capacity for profound change and growth. Let us remember that we are not alone, that we are surrounded by a vast and loving universe that yearns for our highest good. And in each moment, let us choose love, knowing that in doing so, we align ourselves with the very essence of creation itself.

The Energetic Realm

As we traverse this earthly realm, our attention is often fixated on our physical vessels. Indeed, nurturing our physical bodies is crucial, for they serve as the conduits through which we navigate this plane of existence. In our quest for wellness, we also direct considerable focus towards our mental faculties, and yet our ruminating minds often spiral into patterns of chaos. In a previous chapter, we delved into the notion that our minds tend to warp the information they perceive, influenced by the unique lenses through which we perceive the world. Now let's explore the diverse energetic elements influencing our daily existence.

Energy stands as the foundational force propelling every facet of life. Whether it's the rhythm of our heartbeats or the workings of our thoughts, energy manifests in myriad ways, shaping our well-being and perception of reality. To grasp these energies fully, it's crucial to understand the subtle distinctions between physical, mental, emotional, and spiritual energies, recognizing both their specific traits and their interwoven nature.

Symbiotic Energies

◇ **Physical Energy** encompasses the vital force powering bodily functions, movement, and physiological processes, fueling our actions and activities.

◇ **Mental Energy** fuels cognitive processes including thinking, reasoning, problem-solving, and memory, enabling focus, concentration, and intellectual pursuits.

◇ **Emotional Energy** is entwined with our feelings and emotional experiences, shaping mood, motivation, and interpersonal connections.

◇ **Spiritual Energy** pertains to our spiritual practices, connection to something greater, and sense of our purpose in life.

Physical Energy

Physical energy represents the most palpable and universally acknowledged type of energy. It powers the body's biological functions, facilitating movement, metabolism, and essential processes. This energy arises from the nutrients we ingest and the oxygen we inhale, and the processes that transform them into adenosine triphosphate (ATP) through cellular respiration. Physical energy is finite and can fluctuate due to factors such as diet, exercise, rest, and overall health status. It governs our endurance, stamina, and capacity to participate in physical endeavors. Furthermore, physical energy influences our outward appearance, strength, and resilience, mirroring the condition of our body's physiological health.

Mental Energy

Differing from the tangible vitality of physical energy, mental energy refers to the intricate workings of cognition and intellectual engagement. It encompasses the faculties of concentration, focus, memory, creativity, and problem-solving. Mental energy is a cornerstone of cognitive function that is vital for processes such as learning, decision making, and tasks demanding mental acumen. Unlike physical energy, mental energy can be replenished, yet it is also vulnerable to depletion and weariness. Stress, multitasking, and prolonged mental strain are among the factors that can sap mental reserves. Consequently, nurturing mental energy entails mindful practices, prioritization, and periodic breaks to sustain cognitive prowess and stave off burnout.

Emotional Energy

Emotional energy is a vast territory encompassing our feelings, emotions, and how we connect with others. It's the depth and richness of our emotional experiences—whether the highs of joy and love or the lows of sadness, anger, and fear. This energy not only shapes our mood and outlook but also determines how resilient we are in facing life's ups and downs. Unlike physical or mental energy, emotional energy is deeply personal and can shift rapidly in response to both internal and external triggers.

Developing emotional intelligence is key to navigating this dynamic landscape. It involves being aware of, understanding, and managing these fluctuations to foster emotional well-being and enrich our relationships. We foster and gain emotional intelligence by releasing our triggers and moving to a place of equanimity with the data our emotions are giving us.

Spiritual Energy

Spiritual energy flows beyond the confines of the physical, mental, and emotional realms, reaching into the depths of our existence with a profound sense of purpose, connectivity, and transcendence. It touches upon the very core of who we are, resonating with our values, convictions, and our interconnectedness with all that exists in both the physical and spiritual realms. This divine essence intertwines with mindfulness, presence, and inner serenity, guiding us along a path of self-exploration and spiritual enlightenment.

Unlike finite sources of energy, spiritual energy knows no bounds; it is eternal, drawing from the infinite wellspring of consciousness and universal essence. Practices such as meditation, prayer, and reflective introspection nurture this spiritual essence, fostering a harmonious alignment with our higher selves and the expansive cosmos that surrounds us.

In their unique expressions, the energies of the body, mind, emotions, and spirit are intertwined, each affecting and molding the others. Achieving a harmonious equilibrium among these facets is vital for complete well-being and vibrancy. Overlooking any one aspect may result in discord, imbalance, and a sense of discontentment with life. Hence, nurturing mindfulness and purposeful engagement across these realms is crucial for nurturing resilience, satisfaction, and unity within the entirety of our being.

Each energetic dimension contributes uniquely to our overall well-being, functioning, and quality of life. By nurturing these dimensions through conscious practices and self-care, we allow holistic growth, fulfillment, and alignment with our true essence. By learning to recognize and influence this interplay of physical, mental, emotional, and spiritual energy, we unlock the full potential of our being and our ability to accept life's unfolding story with grace and vitality. As you actively engage in this inner work, The Process can be part of a holistic self-care practice helping you nurture yourself from within and transform your life into one where you feel empowered and walk in abundance.

Within each of us lies an innate capacity for growth, healing, and transformation. When we internalize our belief in our ability to nurture our emotional and spiritual energy, a profound shift occurs within us, catalyzing a life of self-discovery and personal evolution. This life transcends mere existence—it encompasses a profound awakening to our true essence and purpose.

As we nurture our emotional and spiritual energies, we embark on a path of self-empowerment and self-realization. Through conscious cultivation and expansion of these energies, we begin to dismantle the barriers erected by self-limiting beliefs that have inhibited our growth and hindered our ability to fully embrace life's boundless possibilities. Confidence emerges as a natural byproduct of this inner nurturing process. When we delve deeper into our emotional and spiritual landscapes, we tap into reservoirs of resilience and strength we never knew we had. With each layer of self-limiting belief shed, we step into the fullness of our being, embracing ourselves with compassion and acceptance.

While we walk our spiritual path with authenticity and integrity, we become living embodiments of our deepest truths and values. Our words and actions align harmoniously with the guiding principles of love, compassion, and wisdom, illuminating the path for others to follow, forging their own paths of self-realization.

Crucially, as we nurture our emotional and spiritual energies, we begin to release the grip of ingrained beliefs and conditioned reactions that have kept us trapped in patterns of behavior incongruent with our authentic selves. We liberate ourselves from the tyranny of societal norms and expectations, reclaiming our sovereignty and autonomy. Central to this transformative process is a profound shift in our worldview. We transition from a perspective rooted in fear, judgment, and separation to one grounded in love, compassion, and interconnectedness. This shift extends beyond mere intellectual understanding; it permeates the very fabric of our being, fostering a deep sense of empathy and unity with all of existence.

Embarking on a journey to understand the diverse dimensions of energy—ranging from the tangible to the intangible—marks a significant step for many. While some may be venturing into this realm for the first time, the notion of interconnectedness between the mind, body, and soul resonates universally. Across cultures and epochs, this triad has remained a focal

Tugging at the Threads of Energy in Your Life

The concept of mind, body, and soul has been a central theme in various philosophical and religious traditions throughout history. When we relate this concept to different forms of energy—physical, mental, emotional, and spiritual—we can see how they interact and contribute to our overall well-being and experience. The mind, body, and soul are interconnected aspects of human existence. When one aspect is out of balance, it can affect the others:

◊ Physical energy can influence our mental and emotional states. For example, physical exhaustion can lead to decreased mental clarity and emotional resilience.

◊ Mental energy plays a role in our physical health and emotional well-being. Chronic stress, for instance, can lead to physical ailments and emotional distress.

◊ Emotional energy impacts both our physical and mental health. Unresolved emotional issues can manifest as physical symptoms or contribute to cognitive difficulties.

◊ Spiritual energy can provide a sense of meaning, purpose, and inner peace, which can positively influence our physical health, mental clarity, and emotional resilience.

Integrating physical, mental, emotional, and spiritual aspects of energy is crucial for holistic well-being. Practices such as utilizing The Process, mindfulness, meditation, exercise, and self-reflection can help balance these energies and promote overall health and vitality. Cultivating a sense of interconnectedness and harmony among these energies can lead to a more fulfilling and balanced life where true transformation occurs.

point in philosophical and religious discourse, embodying the essence of existence itself.

When we extend this paradigm to encompass the realms of physical, mental, emotional, and spiritual energies, a profound labyrinth of inter-connectedness emerges. Each form of energy intricately weaves into the fabric of our being, influencing and shaping our overall well-being and lived experiences.

Transformation can be a profound experience of inner growth and evolution, leading to a spiritual resurrection—a revival of the soul's essence and connection to higher consciousness. As discussed previously, the transformative process often involves shedding old beliefs, patterns, and attachments that no longer serve one's highest good. As individuals confront their inner shadows and embrace vulnerability, they open themselves to deep healing and renewal. Through introspection, self-discovery, and often through challenges or crises, individuals undergo a spiritual metamorphosis, emerging with a renewed sense of purpose, clarity, and authenticity. This resurrection transcends mere change; it signifies a rebirth of the spirit, where we align with our true nature and tap into the universal wisdom that permeates all existence.

At the core of spiritual resurrection is a shift in perception—a profound awakening to the interconnectedness of all life and the recognition of the divine essence within oneself and others. This awakening brings about a sense of unity, compassion, and reverence for the sacredness of existence. As we embody higher states of consciousness, we cultivate qualities such as love, gratitude, and forgiveness, which serve as guiding principles in our interactions with the world. Through this transformation, we not only experience personal liberation but also become agents of positive change, inspiring others to experience their own spiritual resurrections. Ultimately, the process of transformation leading to spiritual resurrection is a sacred pilgrimage, guiding us towards wholeness, liberation, and the realization of our innate divinity.

"Resurrection" is a term most of us are familiar with in religious contexts. However, consider the term in a spirituality connotation. "Resurrection" typically refers to the idea of being reborn or experiencing a renewal of life, often in a spiritual or metaphorical sense. The concept is deeply rooted in various religious traditions, particularly Christianity, where it specifically denotes the rising again of Jesus Christ from the dead. However, beyond its specific religious implications, resurrection can also symbolize a broader spiritual awakening, transformation, or renewal of one's inner being.

In a spiritual context, resurrection may involve renewal or rebirth. In this vein, resurrection can signify a profound transformation or renewal of one's spiritual self, often after a period of struggle, suffering, or spiritual death. It represents emerging from darkness into light, from despair into hope, and from stagnation into growth.

Many spiritual beliefs incorporate the idea of life beyond physical death, where resurrection symbolizes the continuation of consciousness or the soul beyond the limitations of the physical body. Resurrection may also symbolize the attainment of higher spiritual states, such as enlightenment or union with the divine. It represents the awakening of inner potential and the realization of a person's true nature.

In some spiritual traditions, resurrection symbolizes victory over death, not just physical death but also the death of ego, ignorance, and attachment. It signifies transcending the cycle of birth and death by achieving spiritual liberation.

Resurrection in the realm of spirituality encompasses themes of renewal, transformation, transcendence, and the eternal nature of the soul. It offers hope, inspiration, and guidance for us on our spiritual endeavor to find deeper meaning and connection with the divine. Two of the major roadblocks on this spiritual path are triggers and our worldview. By releasing triggers, we renew our worldview and begin to step into grace, becoming a conduit for unconditional love.

In the labyrinth of existence, where our experiences intersect with the echoes of our past and the projections of our future, there exists a profound opportunity for transformation where we can resonate with love and compassion. As we begin to use The Process to release triggers and become conduits for unconditional love, we unearth a newfound appreciation for ourselves and our own souls. This path is not just about extending love outwardly; it is a pilgrimage that leads us inward, to the depths of our being, where the seeds of self-love and liberation await germination.

One of the pivotal revelations on this journey is the realization that as we become vessels of unconditional love, we inevitably nurture a deeper love for ourselves. It is often said that we cannot give what we do not possess. Therefore, to extend boundless love to others, we must first cultivate it within ourselves. We must sometimes work against ego's desires because we must acknowledge the aspects of ourselves that we are embarrassed about and plant seeds of compassion for ourselves first. We reap what we sow, and by sowing self-compassion, we have it to give to others. This isn't about indulging in self-centeredness or egotism, but rather about fostering a healthy, compassionate regard for our own well-being and authenticity.

Through the lens of unconditional love, we experience a resurrection of self—a rebirth into a state of wholeness and acceptance. It is a process of shedding the layers of self-doubt, self-criticism, and self-denial, and embracing the radiant essence of our being. In this state of self-appreciation, we recognize the inherent worth and dignity that resides within us, irrespective of external validations or societal standards. We come to understand that our worthiness is not contingent upon the approval of others but is an intrinsic aspect of our existence.

Loving ourselves in a healthy, non-self-centered manner involves the establishment of boundaries. Boundaries are not barriers to love; rather, they are the guardians of our well-being and self-respect. By setting and honoring boundaries, we assert our right to self-care and create spaces where our authenticity can flourish. This may involve saying no to situations or relationships that compromise our integrity or drain our energy and saying yes to experiences that nourish our soul and align with our highest good.

As we search for self-love and unconditional love, we must walk the talk of our path without resorting to the weaponization of spiritual terms. True spirituality is not about wielding concepts as instruments of power or control; it is about embodying the values of compassion, empathy, and authenticity in our thoughts, words, and actions. It is about living with integrity and humility, and fostering genuine connections rooted in love and mutual respect.

The pilgrimage towards becoming conduits for unconditional love is a sacred odyssey of self-discovery and liberation. It is an undertaking that invites us to embrace the fullness of our being, to love ourselves unconditionally, and to extend that love to others with an open heart and a compassionate spirit. As we navigate this path with courage and grace, may we be guided by the light of unconditional love, illuminating the path towards a more harmonious and interconnected world. We are, after all, a piece of God incarnate.

Engaging in The Process can serve as a powerful instrument in one's journey towards spiritual rejuvenation, self-discovery, and liberation. Through consistent utilization of The Process, we have the opportunity to open ourselves to the possibility of experiencing everyday miracles, whether these manifestations are evident in minor occurrences or in profound, monumental events. It offers a framework to carve out space wherein these miracles can naturally unfold, fostering a deeper connection to the spiritual realm and a heightened sense of awareness in daily life.

Incorporating The Process into your routine not only invites the occurrence of miracles into your life but also emphasizes the significance of integrating these newfound moments of wonder into your being. This integration period is essential for fully comprehending and appreciating the impact of the miracles experienced, allowing you to reflect, absorb, and internalize the lessons inherent in each occurrence. Integration time serves as a crucial pause before you confront and surmount the next significant challenge on your path to spiritual growth.

Recognizing the value of pausing to assimilate these miracles underscores the importance of pacing oneself on the spiritual path. By embracing The Process as a continuous practice rather than a sporadic endeavor, we can navigate our spiritual evolution with greater clarity, purpose, and resilience. Through this cyclical process of experiencing, integrating, and progressing, we can cultivate a deeper sense of fulfillment and alignment with our spiritual essence.

Chapter 6

Faith in the Unseen World

The concept of faith is complex and multifaceted, lending itself to diverse interpretations across various contexts, encompassing religious, philosophical, and personal perspectives. While the nuances of faith may differ, certain recurring elements are often intertwined with the concept.

Belief or trust stands as a foundational pillar of faith—a profound trust or belief in something not necessarily empirically proven or immediately apparent. This could manifest as belief in a higher power, a set of principles, or the fulfillment of specific promises. Confidence in the absence of proof characterizes faith, as it frequently operates in situations where tangible evidence is scarce. It implies a readiness to accept or trust in the existence or occurrence of something based on personal conviction rather than empirical proof.

Faith often carries with it a spiritual or religious dimension, deeply ingrained within various religious customs and beliefs. It embodies a profound trust and conviction in a higher spiritual authority, whether it be a divine entity, cosmic force, or a particular doctrine that guides our understanding of life's meaning and purpose. Yet, faith does not always have a religious connotation behind it.

Personal conviction lends a deeply personal and subjective dimension to faith, involving trust in oneself, others, or the universe. This personal conviction significantly influences decisions, actions, and attitudes. For example, think of the parent who defends their child even when there is empirical evidence they committed a crime. The parent "knows" (has faith) their child is innocent. Or imagine the child who giggles with delight as their parent tosses them into the air, having faith their parent with catch them.

Commitment and devotion are also integral aspects of faith, requiring a level of dedication and dedication to the beliefs or principles of its followers. This commitment may find expression in religious practices, moral values, or a profound sense of purpose. Wars have been fought over people's commitment to their religious practices and the faith they have in their way of life being the right way.

It is crucial to recognize that the meaning and significance of faith can vary significantly among individuals and cultural contexts. While commonly associated with religious beliefs, faith also applies to various facets of life, such as relationships, personal goals, and ethical principles. Additionally, we may place our faith in many types of concepts, including religious doctrines, personal abilities, the inherent goodness of humanity, or the pursuit of meaning and fulfillment in life.

Although faith and hope are often times used interchangeably, they carry distinct meanings and implications. Faith can be succinctly defined as a strong belief or trust in something or someone, often without requiring evidence or proof. On the other hand, hope is characterized by an optimistic expectation or desire for a positive outcome in the future. It entails a sense of anticipation and belief that something favorable will transpire.

Faith is a powerful force that serves as a wellspring of energy for hope. At its core, faith involves a deep-seated belief in something beyond tangible evidence, often rooted in trust, spirituality, or a higher power. This unwavering conviction in the face of uncertainty provides the foundation upon which hope can thrive. When we embrace faith, we tap into a reservoir of strength that enables us to endure challenges and setbacks with resilience.

In times of adversity, faith acts as a guiding light, illuminating the path towards a brighter future. It instills a sense of purpose and meaning, fostering our belief that difficulties are temporary and that positive outcomes are attainable. This positive outlook, fueled by faith, becomes the driving force behind the energy that propels hope forward. Even in the darkest moments, faith becomes the anchor that keeps us grounded and encourages us to look beyond immediate difficulties towards the possibilities that lie ahead.

Furthermore, faith provides us with a sense of connection to something greater than ourselves. This connection transcends personal limitations and instills a collective optimism that extends to the broader community. In shared faith, we find solace and support, creating a network of encouragement that amplifies our energy of hope. Through communal bonds forged by shared beliefs, we draw strength from one another, reinforcing the collective resolve to face challenges head-on and aspire to a better future.

Ultimately, the symbiotic relationship between faith and hope highlights the transformative power of belief. As faith energizes hope, it becomes a dynamic force that propels us and our communities forward, inspiring perseverance, resilience, and a sustained commitment to the pursuit of a brighter tomorrow. In embracing faith, we find not only the strength to weather storms but also the fuel to keep the flame of hope burning brightly.

The realm of spiritual exploration often goes beyond the confines of the physical and plunges into the profound domain of the unseen. Faith in the unseen world serves as a guiding light for those on a spiritual quest, providing comfort, purpose, and a profound connection to mysteries beyond the grasp of the tangible. This steadfast belief in the presence of something beyond our immediate senses is a cornerstone in various spiritual traditions and practices.

At the core of this faith in the unseen lies an acknowledgment that reality encompasses more than what meets the eye. This perspective encourages us to explore the metaphysical, the mystical, and the intangible aspects of existence. It recognizes that the human experience extends beyond the material and includes dimensions that elude our senses and defy easy comprehension.

A fundamental aspect of faith in the unseen is the belief in a higher power or universal intelligence. Whether termed God, the Divine, Source, or by other appellations, this higher consciousness is seen as the conductor of the cosmic symphony, guiding the course of existence with wisdom and purpose. Faith in this unseen force becomes a source of strength, offering solace in challenging times and fostering a sense of confidence in the inherent order of the universe.

The concept of faith in the unseen transcends organized religions and encompasses a broader, inclusive understanding of spirituality. Many spiritual seekers draw inspiration from diverse traditions, ancient wisdom, and personal mystical experiences. In this ecumenical approach, faith becomes a universal language that surpasses religious boundaries, emphasizing the common thread weaving through all paths leading to the unseen.

Your Spiritual Path

Navigating the spiritual path demands a delicate equilibrium between faith and inquiry. While faith encourages trust and surrender to the unseen, inquiry sparks curiosity and a thirst for understanding. The unseen world beckons exploration, and the search for spiritual enlightenment is characterized by an ongoing quest for knowledge, wisdom, and self-discovery. This dynamic interplay between faith and inquiry propels us towards a profound understanding of our spiritual essence.

Faith in the unseen world is a profound recognition of mysteries that surpasses the limits of human perception, inviting spiritual travelers to acknowledge a reality extending beyond the tangible. Through practices, experiences, and an unwavering belief in the existence of the unseen, seekers discover purpose, guidance, and a profound connection to the essence of the divine.

Regardless of whether you consider yourself to be seeking spiritual answers, embracing faith in and connection to the unseen can provide you with the assurance needed to confront challenging decisions, reassuring you that support is ever-present. The tendency to immerse ourselves in human triggers and negative emotions acts as a barrier to our connection with higher consciousness, which we refer to as "God" in the context of this guide to The Process. Releasing emotional triggers enables us to transition to a state of balance with the unseen realm, tapping into a profound vibrational reservoir of knowledge.

Faith & The Process

The Process can serve as a valuable instrument for alleviating the triggers hindering your connections with family and friends. The act of addressing these immediate triggers can, in itself, contribute to leading a more gratifying and enriched life. Yet, the depth to which you explore The Process holds the potential to significantly amplify its impact. By adeptly integrating The Process into spontaneous situations and dedicating time to unraveling entrenched triggers and biases that obscure your worldview, its potency as a life-navigation tool is heightened. In doing so, you cultivate the ability to exist fully in each moment, embodying the most elevated version of yourself. Consequently, The Process evolves into an even more valuable asset in your personal toolkit.

Unleashing the transformative potential of The Process involves recognizing its dual nature. On one level, it serves as a means to liberate us from immediate tensions within relationships, fostering a more satisfying existence. However, the true depth of its effectiveness unfolds when we choose to immerse ourselves in mastering The Process. This mastery involves seamlessly applying it in spontaneous scenarios while concurrently addressing profound, ingrained triggers and prejudices that shape our perception of the world. This multifaceted approach propels The Process beyond a mere problem-solving tool, transforming it into a dynamic force for navigating life with purpose and resilience. As a result, each moment is experienced from the vantage point of your highest self, and The Process emerges as an indispensable asset.

By seamlessly incorporating The Process into impromptu situations and concurrently addressing deep-seated triggers and biases, a profound shift occurs. The expedition towards true self-awakening can feel overwhelming at times. As you move through The Process, you may suddenly feel frustrated or irritated by the questions—and that's perfectly normal!

You're working to change deeply ingrained habits, and your ego won't let them go easily. In those moments, be kind to yourself. Offer yourself love, compassion, and grace, knowing your progress will emerge through a gradual and nuanced exploration. The power of The Process unfolds with greater depth when approached intentionally. While it helps ease surface-level conflicts in relationships and daily life, the most profound transformation awaits those who are willing to explore its deeper layers. By weaving The Process into spontaneous situations and addressing deeply rooted triggers and biases, a significant and meaningful shift can occur.

With each trigger we learn to release, we become better acquainted with our soul, gradually unveiling the authentic essence of who we truly are. Liberated from the whims of our emotions and the potential manipulations by those around us, we evolve into a more buoyant and content version of ourselves. The profound realization we can confidently face any situation, even if triggered or prone to negative emotions, serves as a powerful means of alleviating the apprehension tied to our existence on this planet. It's important to note this transformative process does not promise a life devoid of challenges; rather, it equips us with the capacity to approach life's inherent complexities and uncertainties with a sense of equanimity, enabling us to navigate through them with efficiency and confidence.

The trouble-free existence sought after by many, does not exist. Such a utopian notion remains elusive. However, real power and strength lies in the ability to attain a state of neutrality where we can confront life's inevitable challenges with resilience and poise. This newfound equilibrium does not eliminate obstacles but empowers us to face them head on, transforming each problem into an opportunity for growth. Through this mindset we cultivate a profound sense of inner strength that enables us to traverse the intricate landscape of life with a deeper understanding of ourselves and a resilient spirit.

In essence, the practice of releasing triggers does not shield us from life's problems, but rather it serves as a compass guiding us towards emotional resilience. As we navigate the twists and turns of our lives, The Process facilitates a harmonious relationship with our emotions, allowing us to approach each moment with a grounded and centered demeanor. This

Christy's Story: Experiencing "Pre-Judgement"

During a particular chapter of my life, my husband, our children, and I found ourselves residing in a community where our Protestant faith was not the predominant religious affiliation, especially within our neighborhood. Despite this disparity, my neighbor and I fostered a close bond, overcoming religious differences. She adhered to the prevailing religion of the locality, and our shared experiences involved countless hours engaged in thoughtful walks and conversations.

Religion, a topic often deemed off limits when disparate beliefs come into play, was manifested differently in our connection. Instead of tiptoeing around potential differences, we approached our discussions with an innate curiosity about each other's beliefs. This mutual interest allowed us to explore the intricacies of our respective faiths without the shadow of judgment looming over our conversations.

During one of our many walks, my neighbor divulged an intriguing tidbit. It surfaced that someone from our neighborhood had approached her, inquiring about me. The ensuing conversation took an unexpected turn when the individual remarked, "Christy is genuinely nice, even though she doesn't adhere to our religion," (except she named the religion.) This revelation underscored a prevailing bias within the community, wherein individuals seemingly viewed kindness through the lens of religious conformity.

Rather than being taken aback or offended by this revelation, I reflected on prior encounters. Our real estate agent, belonging to the predominant local faith, had cautioned us about certain neighborhoods, warning that our Protestant affiliation might lead to social exclusion. This echoed the sentiment that kindness was erroneously linked to religious adherence, prompting me to contemplate the broader implications of such preconceived notions within our community. Though at the time I did not have the proper verbiage, this was a prime example of people letting their triggers or lenses cloud their judgement.

transformative process not only enhances our capacity to cope with challenges but also fosters a profound connection with our true selves, leading to a lighter and more fulfilling existence.

With gentleness and understanding, as you incorporate The Process into your practice of self-discovery and personal growth, you enhance your ability to discern the authenticity within situations. It encourages you to distinguish between what truly exists and what may be distorted by your triggers or personal lens. The transformative journey facilitated by The Process facilitates an awakening, introducing the profound notion that awareness eradicates anything that is not genuine.

This seemingly simple yet deeply impactful concept implies that through nurturing a heightened state of awareness, we can gradually uncover and discard the layers of illusion that obscure our perception of reality. This exploration invites us to appreciate the profound influence of awareness, serving as a powerful catalyst for dismantling the "unreal" aspects woven into the fabric of our lives.

Awakening Your Awareness

As we've explored before, the way we experience reality is frequently influenced by our thoughts, emotions, and ingrained beliefs. Our minds craft stories and interpretations that may not always correspond to an absolute truth. The illusions we form may give rise to fears, insecurities, and constraining beliefs, impeding our progress towards personal development and overall well-being.

Teaching ourselves to adhere to the practice of staying attuned to the present moment is a fundamental aspect of personal growth and self-discovery. This entails cultivating mindfulness, where we actively engage in the current moment, observing our thoughts without judgment, and gaining insight into the workings of our consciousness. Through the nurturing of awareness, we sharpen our capacity to differentiate between genuine reality and perceived illusions, thereby deepening our comprehension of life's various encounters.

Removing the veils of illusion involves a compassionate commitment to scrutinize our perceptions and beliefs. As our awareness deepens, we gradually discern the thought patterns that give rise to these illusions. We are empowered to question and eventually dispel them with kindness, understanding, and compassion. These small everyday decisions to empower ourselves opens us to a larger existence of grace along this path of self-discovery.

Embracing awareness grants us the precious gift of aligning our lives with authenticity and staying true to ourselves. As we peel away the layers of illusion, our core values, passions, and purpose come to light. Shedding the burdens of falsehood and living authentically nurtures a profound sense of fulfillment and connection with the genuine aspects of life.

Approaching mindfulness and fostering our ability to evaluate each moment and encounter each moment with an open heart and a non-judgmental attitude unfolds as a transformative odyssey where The Process assumes a pivotal role. Engaging in The Process provides a sanctuary for us to witness our thoughts, emotions, and sensations with a sense of detachment. With consistent practice, it has the potential to nurture an elevated state of awareness, empowering us to gently uncover the layers of societal teachings and conditioned beliefs by lifting the veils that may have obscured their perception in the past.

If just beginning the practice of mindfulness, implementing it into everyday life can be simple and transformative. Start by setting aside just a few minutes each day for focused breathing or meditation, allowing yourself to be fully present in the moment. As you go about your day, try to bring mindful awareness to routine activities—whether you're brushing your teeth, eating a meal, or taking a walk—by paying attention to your senses and surroundings without judgment. Pause for just a moment when performing everyday activities and acknowledge what all your senses are saying about that moment. For instance, what do you hear, see, feel, or taste? Further this practice by pausing to appreciate small moments, like the warmth of the sun or the sound of laughter. Small moments of gratitude bring you into the present moment. Over time, these small acts of mindfulness can help cultivate a deeper sense of peace, clarity, and presence in everything you do. Practicing mindfulness only enhances The Process as it helps us be in tune to ourselves and notice when we become dysregulated.

Mindfulness and The Process go hand in hand. Though the aim of all this internal work is nurturing personal development and fostering a more meaningful life, the principle "awareness dispels the unreal" serves as a compassionate guide. Cultivating heightened awareness empowers us to peel away the layers of illusion, paving the path towards a more genuine fulfilling existence. An added benefit to awakening your own path is that with each step on the path towards self-discovery, you will generate a positive momentum that extends to the well-being of everyone. As we nurture awareness and let go of the unreal aspects of our lives, a ripple effect spreads through our relationships, communities, and the broader world. The collective consciousness gradually shifts towards heightened authenticity, nurturing greater understanding, compassion, and harmony.

Our Soul: the Seat of Self-Love

Embracing awareness enables us to connect with the profound reservoir of our soul. When we delve into the depths of our being at a soul level, we gain the ability to traverse life with a heightened sense of purpose. This empowers us to acknowledge our current position is exactly where we are meant to be. If dissatisfaction lingers in that space, we possess the capacity to instigate change. The exploration of our soul's essence opens the door to cultivating self-love, self-forgiveness, and grace, not only for ourselves but also for those who are part of our lives.

Self-love and self-forgiveness play a crucial role in our journey of self-discovery as they serve as the foundation for building a positive and resilient sense of self. When we value and appreciate ourselves, we create a nurturing environment that fosters personal growth and exploration. This self-compassion acts as a powerful motivator, and grants us the courage to confront challenges, the wisdom to learn from our experiences, and the energy to strive for continuous improvement. Without self-love and self-forgiveness, our path to self-discovery becomes littered with self-doubt and negativity, limiting our ability to authentically explore our true potential.

Furthermore, self-love enables us to establish healthy boundaries and make choices aligned with our values. By recognizing our worth and prioritizing our well-being, we gain the confidence to say no to harmful influences and relationships, as well as distractions that may impede our personal development. This assertiveness and self-respect are essential components of self-discovery, allowing us to sift through external expectations and societal pressures to glean our genuine desires and aspirations.

Ultimately, self-love acts as a catalyst for resilience in the face of setbacks and failures. When we possess a powerful sense of self-worth, we are better equipped to navigate challenges with a positive mindset, viewing setbacks as opportunities for learning and growth rather than insurmountable obstacles or the results of our failures. Expanding our capacity for self-love and self-forgiveness empowers us to cultivate a deep understanding of ourselves, fostering a sense of purpose, authenticity, and fulfillment in our lives. It also moves us closer to recognizing who we are at a soul level.

Souls & Divine Love

In the vast tapestry of existence, there exists a profound and eternal truth—that at our core, we are beings of love at a soul level. This perspective transcends the boundaries of religious doctrines and cultural beliefs, inviting us to explore the idea that we are not merely physical entities navigating the material world but rather energetic manifestations of divine love. According to this worldview, our very essence is derived from the vibration of God: the pure energy of love courses through our spiritual veins.

This profound concept of God as a vibration goes beyond conventional notions of a deity as a distinct entity. It suggests that the essence of the divine is not static or fixed but is instead a dynamic energy that permeates the entire cosmos. In this view, God is not separate from creation but is an intrinsic aspect of it, vibrating at the very core of existence. This perspective invites us to perceive the universe as a symphony of vibrations, with each being and element resonating in harmony with the divine frequency.

To embrace the idea that God is a vibration is to recognize the interconnectedness of all life and the inherent divinity present in every particle of existence. It challenges us to shift our understanding of spirituality from a hierarchical model of worship to one of unity and resonance. Rather than approaching God as an external figure to be supplicated, we are called to attune ourselves to the divine frequency within, aligning our thoughts, actions, and intentions with the loving vibration that underpins all creation. This understanding fosters a deeper sense of reverence for the interconnected web of life and empowers us to co-create a world infused with compassion, harmony, and grace.

The concept that we were created from the vibration of God suggests that at the inception of our existence, we were formed from the very essence of divine love. This divine vibration serves as the energetic blueprint of creation, shaping our souls into vessels of pure, unconditional love. In this paradigm, every individual is an embodiment of the cosmic resonance that emanates from the source of all creation.

Acknowledging that we carry the energetic vibration of God within us signifies that each soul possesses a divine spark. This spark is the radiant core of our being, an eternal flame that connects us to the infinite wellspring of love. As we navigate the complexities of earthly existence, we often find ourselves veiled by the distractions of the material world, obscuring the brilliance of our divine spark. However, learning to recognize and love our true essence involves peeling away these layers and rediscovering the luminosity within. The Process can play a central part in peeling away these layers.

As we gradually release the grip of fear and ego, we create space for the authentic expression of our soul's essence. This process of shedding layers of conditioning and unveiling our true selves is akin to removing the barriers that obstruct the flow of divine love within us. The closer we get to our authentic self at a soul level, the more aligned we become with the inherent love that defines our very existence.

Understanding we are love at a soul level is not just a philosophical concept; it is a transformative realization that calls us to embody this truth in our actions and interactions. When we consciously choose love over fear, compassion over judgment, and kindness over resentment, we are acting out our soul's essence. Through these intentional choices we bring the vibrational frequency of our being into harmony with the divine love that birthed us.

Truly internalizing the idea that at a soul level we are only love, launches us on a profound voyage of self-discovery and spiritual evolution. The recognition of our connection to the divine vibration of God within us serves as a guiding light, illuminating the path towards authenticity and love. As we practice using The Process to release triggers and get closer to who we are at a soul level, we not only align ourselves with the universal energy of pure love but also contribute to the collective awakening of humanity to its divine nature. In this way, the journey towards realizing our true essence—who we are at a soul level—becomes a sacred dance of love as we step in time with the eternal symphony of the universe.

Connecting with Spirit

We've discussed connecting with who we are at a soul level, but what is the difference between soul and spirit? In the realm of spirituality, philosophy, and theology, the concepts of spirit and soul hold significant importance, yet their meanings often overlap, leading to confusion. Distinguishing between these two concepts requires a nuanced exploration of their historical, cultural, and philosophical roots.

"Soul" is the essence of being, and the concept of the soul has deep roots in religious and philosophical traditions worldwide. Traditionally, the soul is regarded as the immaterial essence or core of an individual's being. It is often associated with qualities such as consciousness, identity, emotions, and morality. In many belief systems, the soul is considered eternal, transcending the confines of the physical body. It is sometimes viewed as the seat of one's personality and the repository of experiences and memories.

Throughout history, various perspectives on the soul have emerged. In ancient Greek philosophy, Plato conceived of the soul as a distinct, immortal entity that pre-exists and survives the body. Aristotle, on the other hand, viewed the soul as the animating principle of living beings, encompassing both rational and nutritive aspects.

Unlike the soul, which is often associated with individual identity, the concept of "spirit" is broader and more abstract. Rooted in the Latin word "spiritus," meaning breath or wind, spirit is often understood as a vital force that animates living beings. It is associated with energy, vitality, and consciousness.

In religious contexts, spirit can refer to a divine or supernatural entity, such as the Holy Spirit in Christianity, the Ruach in Judaism, or the Atman in Hinduism. These spirits are often considered manifestations of a higher power or cosmic consciousness.

Spirituality, in this sense, encompasses the pursuit of transcendence, meaning, and connection with something greater than oneself. Furthermore, spirit can denote the inner essence or character of a person. When one speaks of someone having a "spirited" demeanor, it suggests qualities of enthusiasm, vigor, or determination.

While distinctions between spirit and soul are often made, it is essential to recognize these concepts are deeply intertwined and can vary across cultures and belief systems. In some traditions, the terms are used interchangeably, while in others, they denote different aspects of human existence.

Moreover, contemporary interpretations of spirit and soul continue to evolve, influenced by scientific, psychological, and metaphysical insights. Some propose the soul represents the individual's subjective experience and personal identity, while spirit embodies the interconnectedness of all life and the universal consciousness.

In essence, whether you ascribe to the notion of a soul, a spirit, or both, these concepts serve as vehicles for exploring the fundamental questions of human existence, the nature of consciousness, and the mystery of life and death. As we navigate the complexities of existence, understanding the nuances between spirit and soul can enrich our spiritual lives and deepen our appreciation for the profound mysteries of the universe.

In our perspective, spirit embodies the essence within us that directly links to the source. Being attuned to spirit entails experiencing oneness. It flows out through the crown chakra into the vast cosmos, carrying profound wisdom about our origins.

Our spirits serve as the tether to creation. Immersed in spirit, we shed feelings of disconnection, separation, and individuality. Christy and Iris envision spirit as the conduit to non-dual existence. Surrendering to its flow, the sense of "I" dissipates, giving way to a collective "We," a delectable unity. On the other hand, we believe each person's soul is eternal, representing the essence of our being in physical form. It stands in contrast to spirit in several ways, embodying uniqueness amidst the vastness of creation.

When we describe something as "soulful," we often imply depth, intensity, and emotional richness—qualities that are difficult to grasp tangibly and are frequently associated with artistic expression. At the heart of the soul lies a profound sense of individuality, leading us to deeply experience moments of separateness. Hence, when we encounter intense periods, we don't refer to them as "dark nights of the spirit" but rather as "dark nights of the soul." While spirit reaches out expansively into the universe, the soul delves inward, daring to explore the depths of darkness. By acknowledging and confronting our shadows, we reveal the truth of our souls and manifest our courage to traverse these depths.

As we depart from this life, our awareness moves beyond the constraints of our bodies, reuniting with the infinite unity of existence. During this transition, our spirit and soul come together as we release our physical form. This is why we commonly interchange these terms when speaking of connecting with those who have passed away—they symbolize the timeless core of who we are. Understanding this unity helps us see why we often use "spirit" and "soul" interchangeably, especially when considering things from a perspective that sees beyond divisions.

In simple terms, spirit is the energy that links us to the universe, God, and everything intangible, while the soul is our unique essence residing within our human bodies during our time on earth.

From the moment of entering the physical realm, we embark on a quest to discover who we are, often overlooking the profound realization that lies at the core of our being. In the vast tapestry of human existence, we traverse a physical world while filled with questions, seeking purpose and striving to unravel the enigma of identity. We exist in a realm where materialism reigns supreme, where success is measured by external achievements and possessions. Amidst the chaos of daily life, our innate divinity becomes veiled, obscured by the noise of the external world and the illusions of the ego. We spend our entire lives searching for our true selves when, in reality, we are the manifestation of the divine on this earthly plane. To truly embody this essence, we must delve deep within, shedding the layers of conditioning and societal constructs we have collected during our encounters with our physical world.

This process of inner transformation that enables us to live in alignment with this divine vibration requires us to peel back the layers of conditioning that have accumulated over lifetimes, releasing the triggers and traumas that bind us to the illusion of separation. It is a process of surrendering to the inherent wisdom of the heart, allowing its whispers to guide us back to the source of our being. As we tap into our divine wisdom, we come to realize that our identity is not confined to the roles we play or the labels we adopt, but rather transcends the limitations of the egoic mind. We are spiritual beings having a human experience, each endowed with unique gifts and talents, each an expression of the infinite creativity of the divine.

As we attune ourselves to the frequency of divine love, we become vessels for its expression, radiating its light into the world. We no longer seek validation or approval from external sources, for we know that our worth is inherent in our divine essence. Instead, we become beacons of love and compassion, inspiring others to awaken to their own divinity.

With each step on the path of self-discovery, we generate a positive momentum that touches everyone and enhances their sense of well-being. As we nurture awareness and let go of the unreal aspects in our lives, a ripple effect spreads through our relationships, communities, and the broader world. The collective consciousness gradually shifts towards heightened authenticity, nurturing greater understanding, compassion, and harmony.

In embracing our divine essence, we reclaim our power as co-creators of our reality, weaving the threads of love and light into the tapestry of existence. We recognize that we are not merely passive observers, but active participants in the unfolding drama of life. With each thought, word, and action, we have the opportunity to align ourselves with the highest truth of our being, infusing the world with the transformative power of divine love.

Ultimately, self-discovery is not about finding ourselves, but rather remembering who we truly are—divine beings of light and love incarnate. By peeling back the layers of illusion and connecting with the divine within, we awaken to our true nature and fulfill our highest potential. May we all embark on this sacred path with courage and conviction, knowing that the path to liberation lies within the depths of our own hearts. Let The Process be a part of your journey to reconnect with who you truly are.

Chapter 7

Pure Soul & True Essence

We live each of our days as human beings who are doing our best to navigate a physical world that values materialism above all else and uses career achievements and possessions as the surest measure of success. We seek validation from others—family members, friends, loved ones, work colleagues, and sometimes even from strangers on social media. Yet we yearn for more profound meaning in our lives. As a result, from the moment of inception, we embark on a quest to discover who we are, while often overlooking the profound realization that lies at the core of our being—in reality, we are the manifestation of the divine or God on this earthly plane. Amidst the chaos of daily life, this innate divinity becomes veiled, obscured by the noise of the external world and the illusions of the ego. Embedded within the fabric of our consciousness lies the divine spark, the essence of God, pulsating with pure, unconditional love. To truly embody this essence and become an integral part of its cosmic dance, we must delve deep into our inner world, shedding the layers of conditioning and societal constructs that obscure the radiant truth of our existence.

As mentioned earlier in this book, when we begin to unravel the layers of illusion, we come to realize that our identity is not confined to the roles we play or the labels we adopt, but rather transcends the limitations of the egoic mind. We are spiritual beings having a human experience; we are each endowed with unique gifts and talents, each an expression of the infinite creativity of the divine. To live in alignment with this divine vibration requires a process of inner transformation, self-discovery, and spiritual awakening. It is a process of surrendering to the inherent wisdom of the heart, allowing its whispers to guide us back to the source of our being.

As we release triggers and get to a point of neutrality, we are able to connect with the essence of our being—a luminous presence that transcends the limitations of time and space. In this sacred space, we experience the boundless love that flows through us, illuminating every aspect of our existence. We recognize that our true nature is love itself, and that our purpose is to embody this love in all that we do.

When we attune ourselves to the frequency of divine love, we become vessels for its expression, radiating its light into the world. We no longer seek validation or approval from external sources, for we know that our worth is inherent in our divine essence. That burning desire for external validation is extinguished as we become beacons of love and compassion, inspiring others to awaken to their own divinity.

In embracing our divine essence, we reclaim our power as co-creators of our reality, weaving the threads of love and light into the tapestry of human existence. We realize that we are not merely passive observers, but active participants in the unfolding drama of life. With each thought, word, and action, we have the opportunity to align ourselves with the highest truth of our being, infusing the world with the transformative power of divine love.

This odyssey of self-discovery is not about finding ourselves, but rather remembering who we truly are—divine beings of light and love incarnate. By peeling back the layers of illusion and connecting with the divine within, we awaken to our true nature and fulfill our highest potential. May we all embark on this sacred journey with courage and conviction, knowing that the path to liberation lies within the depths of our own hearts.

As we travel through our lives, it is natural to harbor fervent hopes and dreams, each fueled by our individual aspirations and longings. We believe these hopes and dreams are aligned with who we are at a soul level. Yet, amidst this array of desires, it is essential to recognize our personal wishes might not always harmonize with the grand tapestry woven by a higher force. Despite our earnest endeavors to shape events to suit our whims, the will of the divine often reveals a scheme far richer and more benevolent than our finite minds can grasp.

Our innermost desires are shaped by a multitude of factors, weaving together societal norms, cultural backgrounds, and our own deeply held dreams. From the pursuit of material wealth to the quest for recognition, loving relationships, and personal satisfaction, our aspirations are driven by a fundamental human urge to seek fulfillment and ensure our own well-being.

Confronted with the ever-shifting landscape of existence, we frequently find ourselves compelled to exert influence over our surroundings in an effort to shape our desired outcomes. Despite the profound wisdom woven into the fabric of the universe's design, our human nature frequently finds itself at odds with the challenges and hardships the universe presents. In our struggle, we often become ensnared by the grip of our own ego, steadfastly resisting the natural course of life's currents. We adopt various tactics, including setting goals, crafting elaborate plans, and investing unwavering dedication, all in the pursuit of orchestrating circumstances to align with our aspirations. It is a belief rooted in the conviction that we are the architects of our own fate. Yes, we should set goals and work towards them, but we should not become so rigid in how we accomplish those goals that we take away the universe's power to allow miracles to unfold.

It is our tendency to grasp tightly onto our desires, unwilling to recognize the inherent beauty and completeness of the present moment, or to trust in the benevolent guidance of higher forces. Yet, in doing so, we inadvertently intensify our own suffering, descending further into the depths of dissatisfaction and detachment from the interconnectedness of all existence. Our relentless pursuit of these desires often simply traps us in a cycle of chasing external validation and fleeting moments of gratification. This cycle can leave us feeling dissatisfied and empty, as we come to realize that true contentment cannot be found solely in the accumulation of possessions or the approval of others. Fraught with complexities and contradictions, the path to fulfillment is often obscured by the allure of immediate pleasures and societal expectations.

In navigating this confusion of desires, it is crucial to cultivate compassion and understanding for ourselves and others. Recognizing that our wants and needs are deeply intertwined with our humanity, we can approach our aspirations with a gentleness that acknowledges the inherent vulnerabilities and complexities of the human experience. By embracing empathy and kindness, we begin to find a sense of wholeness that transcends the transient allure of external validation and leads us towards a more profound and enduring fulfillment. However, embracing empathy and kindness requires us to release our own personal view of how the world should be.

Surrender & Inquiry

At the heart of our existence lies a profound, tapestry woven by God, often interpreted as the divine will or the grand design of the universe. This transcendent force surpasses our human understanding, flowing beyond the boundaries of time and the constraints of individual desires. It orchestrates the symphony of existence with unparalleled wisdom and intentionality.

Though our aspirations and yearnings may diverge from this celestial blueprint, every step along our path is imbued with significance. Each twist and turn, every triumph and setback, contributes to a greater narrative of growth, enlightenment, and spiritual awakening. In this perspective, we find solace in the understanding that even amidst uncertainty and adversity, we are held within the loving intention of a universal plan that ultimately seeks our highest good. When we tune our frequency to this divine vibration, we are able to surrender our need to control every aspect of our lives and create space for miracles.

Genuine liberation is found in the gentle release of our individual desires, offering them up to the vast wisdom and compassion reverberating through the universe. It is not about giving up or admitting defeat; rather, it is a courageous leap of faith—the belief in the intricate design of our existence by a higher power.

In surrendering, we shed the weight of trying to dictate outcomes or clinging to specific expectations. Instead, we surrender to a profound sense of acceptance, allowing ourselves to be carried by the currents of divine guidance. In this surrender, we discover a boundless realm of potential, where the unfolding of our lives aligns harmoniously with the greater cosmic plan.

Among the complex twists and turns of existence, the dissonance between personal wants and divine will serves as a crucible for spiritual awakening and transformation. As we transcend the limitations of egoic desires and surrender to the guiding hand of the universe, we unveil the inherent beauty and perfection woven into every thread of our existence. Integrating the paradox of personal autonomy and divine orchestration, we navigate the labyrinth of life with grace, humility, and unwavering faith in the benevolent intelligence that guides us towards our ultimate destiny.

In the pursuit of spirituality and embracing the paradox of personal autonomy and divine orchestration, we often encounter various doctrines, beliefs, and dogmas that shape our understanding of the divine. While these constructs can provide structure and guidance, they can also become stumbling blocks if not approached with an open heart and mind. True spirituality transcends rigid adherence to dogma; it is about cultivating a deep connection with the divine and embodying the essence of unconditional love.

"Dogma," by its nature, is a set of beliefs or principles laid down by an authority as indisputably true. While dogmas serve to unify religious communities and provide a framework for understanding the divine, they can also limit spiritual growth and understanding. When we cling rigidly to dogmatic beliefs, we risk closing ourselves off from new insights and perspectives. True spiritual growth requires openness and a willingness to question preconceived notions.

Releasing dogma does not mean abandoning your faith or disregarding sacred texts. Instead, it involves approaching religious teachings with humility and a spirit of inquiry. It requires recognizing that human interpretations of divine truths are inherently limited and subject to error. By releasing dogma, we free ourselves from the constraints of religious orthodoxy and open ourselves to a deeper, more personal relationship with the divine.

At the heart of all spiritual traditions lies the concept of love. Whether it is expressed as compassion, forgiveness, or service to others, love is the essence of spirituality. Walking in the true love of God means embodying this divine love in all aspects of life. It involves cultivating qualities such as kindness, generosity, and empathy and extending them to all beings.

Walking in the true love of God requires a shift in perspective. Instead of viewing God as a distant and judgmental figure, we recognize the divine presence within ourselves and others. We see every interaction as an opportunity to express love and compassion, regardless of religious or cultural differences. In walking in the true love of God, we transcend the boundaries of ego and self-interest, becoming vessels of divine grace and healing in the world.

Moving with her husband's job gave Christy the opportunity to explore a variety of religions and the diverse cultures within them, deepening her understanding of faith. What she discovered was a common thread: everyone sought to walk a path aligned with God. However, after attending numerous churches, Bible studies, and engaging in conversations with people of different faiths, it became clear that many were holding back their ability to love others unconditionally. They seemed to hide behind the dogma of their beliefs, using it as a barrier. Even within their own faiths, people would judge other congregations, question interpretations of sacred texts, or criticize neighbors who followed a different spiritual path. Yet, at the heart of it all, the only true requirement is to ensure that every action is rooted in unconditional love.

Releasing dogma and walking in the true love of God are not mutually exclusive; rather, they are essential and complementary aspects of the spiritual journey. By releasing dogma, we free ourselves from the constraints of religious orthodoxy and open ourselves to new insights and perspectives. We create space for the transformative power of love to flow freely in our lives. Likewise, by walking in the true love of God, we deepen our understanding of spiritual truths and connect more fully with the divine. We embody the essence of spirituality and become agents of divine grace and healing in the world. Through integration, we cultivate a dynamic and authentic relationship with the divine, enriching our spiritual lives and transforming the world around us.

Integration of the two requires a balance between faith and reason, tradition and innovation, discipline and spontaneity. It involves discerning which aspects of religious teachings are life-giving and which are life-restricting. By integrating these insights into our spiritual practice, we cultivate a dynamic and authentic relationship with the divine.

Unconditional Love & Abuse

Though unconditional love and compassion can be our guidingprinciple, it is essential to recognize that embracing this perspective does not equate to passivity or acquiescence in the face of mistreatment.

Central to the understanding of God's unconditional love is the recognition of the complexities within human nature. We acknowledge that people who are suffering may hurt others, often as a result of their own unresolved pain and trauma. Unconditional love prompts us to respond with empathy rather than retaliation, recognizing that beneath the layers of hurt lies a person deserving of love and healing.

However, this understanding should not translate into passivity or acceptance of abusive behavior. While we empathize with the struggles of others, we must also prioritize our own well-being. Just as we extend grace to others, we are equally deserving of respect and dignity. Thus, setting boundaries becomes essential in navigating relationships and interactions.

Understanding that someone may be acting out of fear or hurt doesn't absolve them of accountability. In fact, boundaries can also serve as a catalyst for growth and accountability. By delineating our boundaries, we create opportunities for constructive dialogue and resolution. We invite others to recognize the impact of their actions and take responsibility for their behavior. In doing so, we foster healthier dynamics built on mutual respect and understanding. This balance between empathy and accountability is crucial in fostering healthy relationships and promoting personal growth.

In essence, viewing the world through the lens of God's unconditional love entails both empathy and discernment. It calls us to extend grace to others while also honoring our own worth and well-being. Setting boundaries is not an act of condemnation but rather an act of love—for ourselves and for others. It is a testament to our commitment to cultivate relationships grounded in respect, compassion, and authenticity.

Embracing the perspective of God's unconditional love empowers us to navigate the complexities of human relationships with wisdom and grace. It inspires us to extend compassion to those who are hurting while also valuing ourselves enough to establish healthy boundaries. In doing so, we create spaces where love can flourish, healing can occur, and genuine connections can thrive.

In a world often marred by division, judgment, and prejudice, the concept of viewing life through the lens of God's unconditional love offers a profound vision of a more beautiful existence. Imagine a reality where we all release the triggers that cloud our worldview, allowing everyone to perceive the world and its inhabitants with compassion and understanding. This shift in perspective not only transforms how we interact with others but also holds the potential to revolutionize the very fabric of society. In the ever-evolving landscape of human spirituality and understanding, there emerges a profound shift—an awakening that beckons us to release the chains of dogma and embrace a worldview founded upon the principles of God's unconditional love and boundless compassion. This transformation marks not only a paradigm shift but a revolution of the soul, ushering humanity into a new era of enlightenment and unity.

Unconditional Love

At the heart of this transformative paradigm lies the notion of accepting God's unconditional love. It is a love that knows no bounds, transcending human limitations and prejudices. It sees beyond surface-level differences and acknowledges the inherent worth and dignity of every human being.

In this light, judgments and criticisms lose their power to wound, as they are overshadowed by a profound recognition of the shared humanity that unites us all.

One of the most striking manifestations of this shift is evident in how we respond to the judgments of others. Instead of allowing criticism to inflict pain and diminish our sense of self-worth, we are able to see beyond the surface and recognize the hurting soul behind the judgment. Rather than meeting condemnation with defensiveness or resentment, we respond with empathy and compassion, understanding that the harsh words of others often stem from their own inner turmoil and insecurities.

In embracing God's unconditional love, we cultivate a deep sense of empathy towards our fellow human beings. We recognize that each person carries their own burdens, struggles, and wounds. Rather than perpetuating cycles of hurt and resentment, we choose to extend a hand of kindness and understanding. We become beacons of light in a world too often shrouded in darkness, offering hope and healing to those in need.

Viewing the world through the lens of God's unconditional love empowers us to break free from the shackles of prejudice and discrimination. We no longer define others based on superficial characteristics such as race, religion, or socioeconomic status. Instead, we see each individual as a beloved child of the Divine, deserving of love, respect, and dignity. In doing so, we dismantle barriers that divide us and foster a sense of unity and interconnectedness among all people.

This shift in perspective not only transforms individual lives but also has the power to catalyze broader social change. As more and more of us embrace the principles of unconditional love and compassion, each of us becomes an agent of transformation within our community. Acts of kindness, empathy, and forgiveness ripple outward, creating a ripple effect of positivity and healing that reverberates throughout society.

The world envisioned through the lens of God's unconditional love is one of unparalleled beauty and harmony. It is a world where judgments are replaced with compassion, where divisions are bridged by empathy, and where love reigns supreme. While achieving such a reality may require a profound shift in consciousness, the rewards are immeasurable. As we release the triggers that cloud our worldview and open our hearts to the transformative power of love, we pave the way for a brighter, more compassionate future for all.

In a world often tumultuous and fraught with pain, the concept of viewing it through the lens of God's unconditional love offers a beacon of hope and understanding. It beckons us to see beyond the surface, to recognize the inherent value in each individual, and to approach all situations with compassion and grace.

Motivations: Justice Versus Revenge

Viewing the world through the lens of unconditional love does not mean we don't hold others accountable for their actions. In the annals of human history, the concepts of justice and revenge have often been conflated, misunderstood, or even used interchangeably. However, a nuanced examination reveals they are fundamentally distinct, not only in their objectives but also in the motivations and energies that drive them.

At its core, justice is a principle grounded in fairness, accountability, and the restoration of balance within society. It operates within a framework of established laws, moral codes, and ethical standards, seeking to ensure that we are all are held responsible for our own actions, and the rights of all are upheld. Justice, in its purest form, is impartial, objective, and seeks to rectify wrongs without succumbing to personal biases or vendettas.

One of the distinguishing features of justice is its capacity for compassion and empathy. While it demands accountability, it also recognizes the humanity of both the perpetrator and the victim. True justice acknowledges the suffering inflicted upon the victim and strives to address their needs for restitution, healing, and closure. Moreover, it aims to rehabilitate the offender, offering opportunities for redemption and reconciliation, thereby fostering a sense of unity and cohesion within society.

In stark contrast, revenge is driven by the toxic energies of anger, hatred, and a desire for retribution. Unlike justice, which operates within established legal and moral frameworks, revenge operates outside the boundaries of reason and restraint. It is a primal urge, fueled by the need to inflict pain and suffering upon those perceived as wrongdoers, often without regard for the consequences or the principles of fairness.

Revenge is a cyclical and self-perpetuating cycle that breeds further violence and animosity. It feeds on itself, consuming not only the object of vengeance but also the person seeking it. Far from bringing closure or resolution, revenge only deepens wounds, perpetuating a cycle of conflict and suffering that echo through generations.

Justice and revenge are two fundamentally different concepts that operate on opposing principles and energies. Understanding the distinction between justice and revenge is essential for the maintenance of a just and harmonious society. While justice seeks accountability, fairness, and restoration, revenge is driven by hatred, anger, and a desire for retaliation. Ideally, justice seeks to address grievances through lawful and compassionate means, whereas revenge only serves to perpetuate cycles of violence and division. Societies can pave the way for a more compassionate, equitable, and harmonious world by using principles of justice and rejecting the lure of revenge.

Divine Love Is a Beacon for Hope

When Christy and Iris work with others when mentoring or coaching, this question invariably finds its place in our conversations: What is your motivation? It is a simple inquiry, yet its implications run deep, shaping the very essence of our actions and decisions. It serves as a compass, directing our focus towards the core of their intentions and desires. By exploring the energy behind their actions, we uncover profound truths about their inner workings.

Motivation serves as the driving force behind every action we take, illuminating our path and influencing our journey's outcome. As a mentor or coach, understanding the motivations of those we guide is paramount, as it provides invaluable insight into our mentees' aspirations, values, and potential pitfalls.

Consider the emotions that accompany your actions. Are they fueled by anger and hatred, or do they emanate from a place of understanding and compassion? The energy we invest in our endeavors reveals volumes about our motivations and the paths we tread. When caught up in our own triggers, it is difficult to step back and evaluate the situation from a place of neutrality. Neutrality is where we can tap into our own soul's wisdom without being lost in the deluge of emotions overtaking us.

Anger and hatred, while potent emotions, often lead us astray, clouding our judgment and steering us towards paths fraught with conflict and despair. When these emotions overshadow our intentions, they poison our interactions and sabotage our progress. It is crucial to recognize these warning signs and guide ourselves towards a more constructive mindset.

Conversely, actions fueled by understanding and compassion pave the way for growth and enlightenment. When we approach challenges with an open heart and a genuine desire to help others, we align ourselves with a spiritually blessed path. Our actions become a beacon of hope, inspiring those around us to practice empathy and kindness in their own lives. As we navigate the complexities of human interaction, let us never forget the power of motivation to shape our destinies. By fostering understanding and compassion in our hearts, we can illuminate the path ahead and guide others towards a brighter, more fulfilling future.

In the complexities of existence, humans are often caught between two realms: the worldly and the spiritual. The dichotomy between being in the world and not of the world has been an enduring theme across cultures, religions, and philosophical traditions. At its core lies a profound truth about the human condition and the quest for inner harmony and enlightenment.

To be in the world implies active participation in the daily affairs of life—engaging with society, pursuing ambitions, and navigating the complexities of human relationships. However, to be of the world leads to a deeper attachment to materialism, ego-driven desires, and a sense of separation from the divine essence. The importance of aligning with one's soul and embodying unconditional love becomes apparent within this delicate balance of worldliness and inspiration.

Every moment presents a choice—to perpetuate the cycles of suffering and separation or to choose the path of compassion and unity. This choice reverberates not only within our own lives but also throughout the interconnected web of existence. By consciously choosing love over fear, kindness over indifference, people contribute to the elevation of consciousness and the realization of a more harmonious world.

The importance of being in the world, not of the world, lies in its potential to empower us to transcend the limitations of the egoic mind and awaken to the boundless nature of the soul. It is a journey of integration—integrating the mundane with the sacred, the personal with the universal, and the finite with the infinite. In this sacred union, we become conduits of divine grace, channeling love and wisdom into the flow of reality.

Being in the world, not of the world, does not imply detachment or renunciation of worldly responsibilities. Instead, it invites a shift in perspective—viewing worldly pursuits and challenges through the lens of spiritual evolution and divine purpose. Whether in moments of joy or adversity, we are invited to cultivate a deep sense of presence and mindfulness, anchoring ourselves in the eternal now where the essence of God's love resides.

In essence, the importance of being in the world, not of the world, lies in its capacity to awaken humanity to its highest potential—to live in alignment with the truth of who we are as beings of love and light. As each of us embraces our divine essence and chooses the path of love, we contribute to the collective awakening of consciousness, paving the way for a world infused with compassion, harmony, and peace. When used with intention and purpose, The Process can be a navigating light on this path of compassion, harmony, and peace.

By awakening our own inner light, we learn to serve humanity. In the history and future of human existence, the concept of serving humanity stands as a beacon, igniting the very essence of our souls. Through acts of kindness, compassion, and selflessness, we not only uplift others but also nourish our own spirits. However, amidst the noble endeavor of serving others, it is imperative to achieve an elusive balance between altruism and self-care. For our souls to truly ignite in service, we must not forget the importance of establishing boundaries and nurturing self-love. After all, we cannot pour from an empty cup; we must first fill ourselves with love and compassion before we can extend it to others.

Self-Love & Boundaries

When we engage in acts of service to humanity, whether it be volunteering at a local shelter, lending a helping hand to a neighbor in need, or advocating for social justice causes, we tap into the deepest recesses of our humanity. The connection forged through service transcends individual differences and cultivates a sense of unity and interconnectedness. In these moments, our souls are ignited with a profound sense of purpose and fulfillment as we witness the positive impact of our actions on the lives of others.

While the impulse to serve others is undoubtedly noble, it is essential to recognize the significance of setting boundaries in all aspects of our lives, including volunteering and serving others. Boundaries serve as protective barriers that safeguard our emotional and mental well-being. Without them, we risk burnout, resentment, and ultimately, the inability to continue serving effectively. Establishing boundaries means honoring our limitations, learning to say no when necessary, and prioritizing self-care without guilt or shame. By doing so, we create a sustainable foundation from which to continue serving humanity with authenticity and compassion.

At the heart of genuine service lies a deep reservoir of self-love. Just as a flame cannot burn without fuel, we cannot sustainably give love and support to others if we neglect to love ourselves first. Self-love is not selfish; it is a fundamental prerequisite for authentic service. When we prioritize self-love, we replenish our inner reserves of compassion, kindness, and empathy, enabling us to give wholeheartedly without depletion. Moreover, by modeling self-love, we inspire others to cultivate a similar sense of worthiness and empowerment.

Derek Price, a distinguished British physicist, historian of science, and information scientist, once made an intriguing observation within the realm of academia. He discerned a recurring pattern where a select few individuals consistently dominated the landscape of scholarly publications within their respective fields. This observation eventually crystallized into what is now known as Price's law: that 50 percent of the work is typically shouldered by the square root of the total number of participants involved.

Boundaries with Loved Ones

Many of us have become adept at extending ourselves to others, mastering the art of giving without restraint. Yet, what often eludes us is the ability to establish healthy boundaries. Christy recalls that when her children were young, her days were a whirlwind of activity, from overseeing their extracurricular clubs to volunteering within her community and supporting her husband's endeavors at his workplace, all while maintaining the balance of household duties, meal schedules, and working the job that paid her for her labor. In the midst of this ceaseless giving, Christy found herself harboring a simmering resentment towards those who seemed oblivious to the concept of pitching in.

As she awakened her path, she realized that boundaries serve as protective measures, safeguarding our emotional, mental, and physical health. They communicate our limits and establish expectations for acceptable behavior. Contrary to misconceptions, setting boundaries is not an act of selfishness but rather an act of self-care and self-respect. It is a declaration that we value ourselves enough to refuse to tolerate mistreatment or disrespect.

As Christy and Iris reflected on this phenomenon, we wondered whether a more conscious exploration of boundaries and self-care could serve to rebalance this skewed ratio as more people would channel their energies into endeavors that each person is more attuned to. It is paramount to engage in activities that emanate from a place of genuine passion and fulfillment. If cooking brings you joy, consider channeling that passion towards preparing nourishing meals for ailing neighbors or lending a helping hand at a local soup kitchen. Alternatively, if your strength lies in being a compassionate listener, offer your empathetic ear to those who may be yearning for connection, whether it is a friend in need or individuals within a volunteer organization. Ultimately, the key lies in aligning our actions with our authentic selves and operating from a space of heartfelt intention. By doing what we love, imbued with genuine care and compassion, we not only enrich our own lives but also contribute meaningfully to the well-being of others and truly serve humanity.

The essence of serving humanity is not merely individual pursuits but collective service. When we extend our efforts beyond personal gain and commit to uplifting not only ourselves but also humanity, a profound transformation occurs within us. This transformation ignites our light body, setting ablaze the dormant sparks of divinity within, and propels us towards a more profound alignment with the cosmic forces that govern our universe.

Central to this metamorphosis is the realization that true fulfillment emanates from serving a purpose greater than ourselves. When we fully internalize this principle, we embark on a sacred quest to channel our energies towards acts of compassion, kindness, and selflessness. By recognizing the interconnectedness of all beings, we acknowledge our inherent responsibility to contribute positively to the collective tapestry of existence. In doing so, we unlock the latent potential within us, transcending the limitations of ego and material desires.

To walk the path of service is to embody the essence of love in its purest form. It is a journey that begins with the cultivation of a heart-centered consciousness—a state where empathy, compassion, and benevolence become the guiding principles of our existence. Yet, to reach this state of being, we must first confront the shadows that obscure our vision and hinder our ability to perceive the world through the lens of unconditional love.

These shadows, often manifested as egoic attachments, fears, and insecurities, are barriers that separate us from our divine essence. They cloud our perception, distorting our worldview and perpetuating a cycle of separation and discord. However, through introspection and conscious awareness, we can begin to recognize these triggers, releasing ourselves from their grip and reveling in a more expansive perspective rooted in love and unity. The Process can be an important part of this transformation when used consistently.

As we relinquish the shackles of our conditioned beliefs and societal constructs, we open ourselves to the transformative power of service. It is through acts of kindness, generosity, and altruism that we align ourselves with the divine flow of the universe, becoming vessels for the manifestation of its infinite love and wisdom. In extending a helping hand to those in need, we not only uplift their spirits but also illuminate our own path, for in serving others, we serve the highest expression of our own soul. These acts can be as mundane as being kind to the checkout person at the grocery store when we are feeling cranky at our children for misbehaving the entire time we were shopping or acting with forgiveness towards the person who cut us off in traffic.

The ripple effects of our actions extend far beyond the confines of our immediate reality, weaving a tapestry of interconnectedness that reverberates throughout the cosmos. Each act of service, no matter how small, contributes to the collective evolution of humanity, igniting a chain reaction of love and compassion that knows no bounds.

Becoming of service to ourselves and those around us is a sacred pilgrimage towards the realization of our divine essence. It is a path illuminated by the radiant light of unconditional love, where each step brings us closer to the eternal source from which we all originate. By releasing the triggers that cloud our lens and embodying a heart-centered consciousness, we align ourselves with the cosmic forces of creation, becoming beacons of hope, healing, and transformation in a world yearning for the light of divine love. Remember to be of service to yourself first and that self-love will naturally overflow to those around you and the choices you make in everyday life.

Chapter 8

Self-Love,
Boundaries & Neutrality

In the previous chapters, we explored the profound significance of service and its inseparable connection with love. We delved into the essence of service as the embodiment of love in its purest form. However, as we seek a path through the intricacies of service and love, we inevitably encounter a fundamental truth: we cannot give what we do not possess. This truth echoes through the corridors of wisdom, reminding us of the paramount importance of self-love as the precursor to genuine service.

As we draw nearer to the conclusion of this book, our exploration culminates in a vital realization—that before we can extend unconditional love and service to others, we must first cultivate unconditional love within ourselves. This realization will be your cornerstone as you build your connection to the divine through authentic service, and it underscores the significance of self-care, self-compassion, and self-nurturing.

Self-love, often misconstrued as a selfish or indulgent concept, is, in fact, the basis of personal growth and altruistic endeavors. It is the foundation upon which our capacity to love and serve others rests. Just as a tree draws nourishment from its roots before bearing fruit, we must nourish our inner selves with love and kindness before extending our branches outward.

In the hustle and bustle of modern life, the concept of self-love can often become obscured amidst the demands of work, relationships, and societal expectations. We may find ourselves caught in a relentless cycle of striving for external validation, neglecting the whispers of our own hearts yearning for self-acceptance and compassion. However, true fulfillment and service spring forth from a wellspring of self-love that flows deep within us, nourishing every aspect of our being.

The journey towards self-love is not a linear path but a dynamic process of self-discovery and growth. It requires us to confront our inner demons, accept our vulnerabilities, and celebrate our inherent worthiness. It beckons us to cultivate a nurturing relationship with ourselves, characterized by self-respect, self-forgiveness, and self-empowerment.

The practice of self-love encompasses various dimensions of our being—our physical, emotional, mental, and spiritual energies. It involves honoring our bodies with nourishing food, restorative rest, and rejuvenating movement. It entails nurturing our emotional well-being through self-expression, mindfulness, and healthy boundaries. It requires tending to our mental landscape with self-awareness, positive affirmations, and constructive self-talk. And it invites us to deepen our spiritual connection through contemplation, meditation, and acts of reverence towards ourselves and the universe.

The construct of self-love requires us to awaken our individual path of personal growth and liberation, marked by the release of triggers, the transformation of our worldview, and the emancipation from societal dogma. It beckons us to courageously confront every aspect of ourselves, both light and shadow, in order to know our true essence. This path is not for the faint hearted; it requires resilience, vulnerability, and an unwavering commitment to self-discovery and self-acceptance.

Releasing triggers is a pivotal aspect of the self-love journey, as it involves untangling ourselves from the past wounds and conditioning that hold us captive. Triggers, often rooted in unresolved trauma or limiting beliefs, can thwart our ability to experience genuine self-love and fulfillment. By acknowledging and addressing these triggers with compassion and courage, we pave the way for profound healing and transformation.

Self-love entails a radical shift in our worldview—a departure from societal norms and expectations that may have dictated our sense of worth and identity. It challenges us to question inherited beliefs and narratives that no longer serve our highest good, empowering us to forge our own path based on authenticity and self-trust. This process of liberation requires us to be brave enough to challenge the status quo and embrace the fullness of our being, free from external validation or conformity.

Setting ourselves free from societal dogma is a courageous act of reclaiming our autonomy and sovereignty. It involves deconstructing the cultural conditioning and social constructs that have shaped our self-perception and behavior, allowing us to rediscover our inherent worthiness and power. By dismantling these layers of external influence, we create space for our authentic selves to emerge, liberated from the confines of societal expectations.

Following your path of self-love is not a quick fix or linear process; rather, it is a multifaceted endeavor that unfolds over time. It requires patience, perseverance, and the utilization of various tools and practices—from therapy and journaling to meditation and self-care rituals. The Process, in particular, can serve as a central part of this journey, giving you a structured framework for peeling back the layers of conditioning and unveiling the truth of who we are. Through introspection, reflection, and inner work, you will gradually align with your authentic self, embodying the essence of self-love and living from a place of wholeness and integrity.

Self-love is fundamentally not a static endpoint but rather an ongoing odyssey to be welcomed—an expedition of self-exploration, restoration, and metamorphosis. It stands as a revolutionary act of self-compassion, liberating us from the chains of self-doubt and inadequacy, thereby enabling us to radiate our inner brilliance in the world.

Self-love paves the way for authentic service to others, for it is only when we are filled to the brim with love and compassion for ourselves that we can overflow with abundance, generously sharing our gifts with those around us. Our acts of service become infused with authenticity, humility, and empathy, emanating from a place of wholeness and integrity.

Cultivating self-love enables us to navigate the complexities of life with grace and resilience. It equips us with the inner resources to weather storms, overcome challenges, and recognize our inherent worthiness, regardless of external circumstances. In doing so, we become beacons of hope and inspiration, illuminating the path for others as they progress towards self-love and service.

As we approach the culmination of our exploration, let us remember that the path of service begins within. Before we can extend the hand of compassion to others, let us first extend it to ourselves. Let us embark on the journey of self-love with courage, gentleness, and unwavering commitment, knowing that this is how we build our ability to love and serve others. As we embody the essence of self-love, may we become radiant vessels of love and service, illuminating the world with our boundless compassion and grace.

Exploring self-love is akin to setting sail into uncharted waters, where the winds of transformation propel us towards a destination of self-awareness and acceptance. In this odyssey, various tools and practices become our compass, guiding us through the ebbs and flows of our inner landscapes. Among these tools, The Process emerges as an essential part, offering a roadmap towards self-discovery and healing. However, alongside these tools, there exists a fundamental cornerstone that cannot be overlooked: the setting of healthy boundaries.

Boundaries

In the pursuit of self-love, creating and maintaining healthy boundaries becomes paramount. Intentional boundaries help us draw lines in the sand and delineate where we end and others begin, safeguarding our emotional, mental, and physical well-being. Setting healthy boundaries is not an act of selfishness or rudeness, as some may misconstrue, but rather an act of self-preservation and compassion—both for oneself and others.

Boundaries serve as the delineation of acceptable behavior, offering a clear roadmap for navigating our interactions with others. By articulating what is permissible and what isn't, we create a framework wherein we feel respected, valued, and secure. This act asserts our autonomy and affirms personal agency in shaping relationship dynamics. Furthermore, setting boundaries communicates a profound message of self-worth—it declares that our needs and emotions are valid and deserving of acknowledgment.

At the heart of boundary-setting lies the recognition that honoring our own worth and well-being is not only our right but also our responsibility. It is a deliberate act of self-care, rooted in the understanding that we are worthy of love, respect, and dignity. This declaration of self-respect signals to the world that we refuse to compromise our authenticity or sacrifice our needs on the altar of external expectations. When we set boundaries, we send a powerful message to ourselves—and to the world—that our worth is non-negotiable and that we deserve to be treated with kindness, empathy, and understanding. Thoughtfully establishing boundaries creates a sanctuary within which our true selves can flourish, shielded from the onslaught of toxicity and negativity that often pervades our relationships and environments.

Crucially, the act of setting boundaries does not entail demanding others to change or conform to our expectations. Instead, it entails granting others the freedom to be themselves while simultaneously safeguarding our own emotional well-being. It is an act of detachment from the responsibility of managing others' behaviors and choices, allowing us to relinquish the burden of trying to control external circumstances. In essence, setting boundaries is an act of self-empowerment rooted in the belief that we each possess the agency to shape our own reality.

Boundary-setting is a practical tool in the arsenal of self-love, but it requires courage and conviction to assert our needs and set our limits, especially in a society that often glorifies self-sacrifice and martyrdom. Yet, it is precisely through the establishment of boundaries that we reclaim our agency and craft our narrative, steering our lives down a path of authenticity and fulfillment.

Setting boundaries is not a one-time endeavor but rather an ongoing practice that progresses as we grow and evolve. It necessitates regular self-reflection and recalibration to ensure boundaries remain aligned with our own values and needs. As we continue our exploration of self-love, we may encounter setbacks and obstacles, but it is through these experiences we gain invaluable insights into our own strength and resilience.

Setting healthy boundaries is a pivotal aspect of this journey, a powerful tool that gives us resilience to navigate the complexities of relationships and emotions.

Though establishing and enforcing boundaries in relationships is a crucial aspect of maintaining emotional health and fostering mutual respect, this process is not without its hurdles. It demands courage, self-awareness, and a readiness to confront discomfort head-on. When asserting our boundaries, we often find ourselves grappling with various challenges, particularly in situations where boundaries have been previously disregarded or undermined. One of the primary challenges of setting boundaries in relationships is the emotional turmoil and vulnerability it can evoke. It requires us to confront our own needs and assert them, which can be an uncomfortable and daunting task. We may experience feelings of guilt or fear of rejection when expressing our boundaries, especially if we expect negative reactions from people we have a connection to.

If we have been in a relationship where boundaries have been previously absent or disregarded, we may struggle even more profoundly with these emotions. We may question the validity or value of the boundaries we are setting, fearing that asserting them will lead to conflict or even the dissolution of the relationship. This fear of abandonment or disapproval can prevent us from asserting our needs authentically, leading to a cycle of self-neglect and resentment.

Another significant challenge in setting boundaries within relationships is the potential for resistance and pushback from partners. When we establish boundaries for the first time with someone who is accustomed to having free rein, it can trigger a defensive reaction. Partners may feel threatened or rejected by the introduction of boundaries, interpreting them as a sign of distrust or dissatisfaction with the relationship.

This resistance can manifest in several ways, ranging from subtle manipulation to outright defiance. Partners may attempt to invalidate or minimize the importance of the boundaries, "gaslighting" or tricking us into questioning our own perceptions or needs. They may resort to guilt-tripping or emotional blackmail, leveraging past behavior or affection to coerce us to comply with their wishes.

Setting boundaries, especially in relationships where they have been absent or disregarded, often triggers inner conflict and self-doubt. We may wrestle with feelings of ambivalence, torn between the desire to assert our needs and the fear of causing disruption or disappointment. This internal struggle can erode our confidence and undermine our resolve, making it challenging to maintain boundaries consistently.

Moreover, we may doubt the validity of our boundaries, particularly if we have internalized the expectations others have of us to prioritize others' needs over our own. We may question whether our boundaries are reasonable or fair, second-guessing our right to assert them. This self-doubt can be exacerbated by the other person's reactions, further complicating the process of boundary-setting, and reinforcing feelings of inadequacy.

While setting boundaries in relationships undoubtedly presents numerous challenges, we can employ strategies to navigate them effectively. Cultivating self-awareness is an essential precursor to effectively setting boundaries in any relationship. Before delineating boundaries, it is crucial to engage in introspection, reflecting on your individual needs, values, and limits. This process involves deepening your understanding of yourself, discerning what holds significance, and recognizing the boundaries necessary for maintaining mental, emotional, and physical health. By gaining clarity on personal values and motivations, you can articulate boundaries that align with your authentic self and promote mutual respect. Understanding the importance of setting boundaries for your well-being empowers you to assert your needs confidently and navigate relationships with integrity and authenticity.

Next, clear and assertive communication is paramount. It is essential to express your boundaries using straightforward and direct language that leaves no room for ambiguity. Being assertive but respectful in your communication ensures that your needs are effectively conveyed without diminishing the other person's feelings or autonomy. By emphasizing the importance of boundaries in fostering a healthy and mutually respectful relationship, you underscore their significance in maintaining balance and harmony. Clear and assertive communication lays the foundation for mutual understanding and collaboration, enabling everyone affected to navigate the relationship with transparency and integrity.

Setting consequences and adhering to them is also a critical aspect of boundary-setting within relationships. It involves clearly communicating the repercussions of crossing established boundaries and being prepared to follow through on those consequences if necessary. Consistency is paramount in upholding boundaries and ensuring their integrity. By establishing predictable outcomes for boundary violations, you reinforce the importance of respecting each other's limits and promote accountability within the relationship. Ensuring that each person understands and participates in discussions about the boundaries and the consequences of crossing them fosters a sense of mutual respect and trust. Ultimately, setting and enforcing consequences serves to uphold the integrity of boundaries and cultivate healthier, more balanced relationships.

Seeking support is another crucial step in navigating the challenges of boundary-setting within relationships. Whether it's confiding in trusted friends, family members, or seeking guidance from a therapist, reaching out for support can provide valuable validation and encouragement. Surrounding yourself with individuals who respect and understand the importance of prioritizing self-care can give you a better sense of perspective and bolster your confidence in asserting your boundaries. Through open communication and empathetic listening, supportive networks can offer insights and strategies for effectively navigating difficult conversations and maintaining boundaries. By leaning on these supportive relationships, you can gain the strength and reassurance needed to uphold your boundaries and cultivate healthier, more fulfilling relationships.

Practicing self-compassion is an essential aspect of navigating the ambiguities of setting boundaries within relationships. It involves extending kindness and understanding to yourself, especially during moments of discomfort or vulnerability. Recognizing that it's natural to feel uneasy when asserting boundaries, you can cultivate a sense of gentleness towards yourself. Prioritizing your own needs is not selfish but rather a fundamental aspect of self-care and well-being. By embracing self-compassion, you can foster resilience and inner strength, empowering yourself to assert boundaries confidently and navigate relationships with authenticity and integrity.

Setting boundaries in relationships is often accompanied by a myriad of challenges, ranging from emotional discomfort to fear of conflict. However, despite these obstacles, it remains an indispensable aspect of self-care and personal growth. Confronting discomfort head-on and asserting our needs is essential for fostering emotional well-being and maintaining healthy relationships. Through the process of boundary-setting we can establish a foundation of self-respect, recognizing and honoring our own worth in the dynamics of interpersonal connections. Using The Process at any point while setting boundaries can be an invaluable tool in releasing the behavior that prevents us from setting healthy boundaries.

Ultimately, learning to set boundaries provides us with an opportunity for profound personal growth and lays the groundwork for cultivating healthier and more fulfilling relationships. By working through the complexities of asserting boundaries, we develop resilience and self-awareness. We learn to advocate for ourselves effectively while also respecting the boundaries of others, fostering a culture of mutual respect and understanding within relationships. Through this process, we not only strengthen our sense of self but also cultivate deeper connections with those around us. Embracing the discomfort of boundary-setting is a transformative endeavor that enables us to nurture authentic connections based on honesty, empathy, and mutual support.

As we continue on our path towards enlightenment, whether setting boundaries or shedding triggers, it becomes necessary to master the art of achieving a state of neutrality, which can also cause discomfort that we need to learn to confront. The relentless pursuit of pleasure and avoidance of discomfort have become ingrained in the fabric of modern society, making the idea of embracing neutrality a daunting prospect for many. In a world inundated with instant gratification and perpetual stimulation, the concept of neutrality can seem like an elusive ideal.

Neutrality

At the heart of The Process lies the aspiration to achieve a state of neutrality. This state rises above the chaotic fluctuations of our minds and emotions, offering a vantage point from which we can perceive the world with clarity and compassion. Neutrality endows us with the capacity to observe events without being engulfed by their emotional

Iris Receives an Unexpected Gift

For most of my life, anxiety was my motivator. It pushed me to succeed, especially in the high-pressure world of corporate America. But while writing this book, I had an anxiety attack because I felt my work on The Process was not moving fast enough, and that's when I realized it was time for anxiety to go. It just wasn't serving me anymore.

When I released the trigger of anxiety, I was left with something I didn't expect: emptiness. It was a strange, uncomfortable feeling that completely caught me off guard. I remember waking up the next day, feeling like I was mourning the loss of an old friend. There was a deep sadness, a sense of melancholy, and I couldn't help but wonder, "What do I do now?"

To process what I was experiencing, I sat down and made a list. I wrote out all the ways anxiety had helped me—pushing me to be productive and focused—but also how it had hurt me and my health and controlled my life. As I worked through this list, I remembered something crucial: in my life, whenever the universe takes something away, it always replaces it with something better.

Even when we lose something that's been harmful, it's still a loss. We need to give ourselves the time, grace, and space to mourn. Letting go of anxiety wasn't just about reducing stress; it was about honoring the space that opened up and trusting that something better would eventually fill it.

It took about a week for me to notice the lightness. I wasn't driving with aggression anymore, overreacting, or sweating the small stuff. Instead, I felt a kind of freedom I had never experienced before. It was as if, in releasing anxiety, I had finally made room for peace.

undertow, empowering us to respond thoughtfully rather than react impulsively. It is a state of equilibrium where inner peace and outer chaos coexist harmoniously. Yet, in our contemporary landscape dominated by instant gratification and constant stimulation, achieving neutrality is fraught with challenges. The incessant barrage of stimuli leaves little room for introspection and stillness. In a culture that values busyness and productivity more than anything else, peace and calm can feel like foreign concepts. The discomfort of silence and solitude is often met with resistance, driving us to seek solace in distractions and superficial pleasures.

For many of us, the prospect of living in a state of neutrality can be unsettling. The very notion of relinquishing the highs and lows of emotional turbulence can evoke feelings of apprehension, resistance, and emptiness. After all, we have been conditioned to equate intensity with significance, and neutrality can appear dull and lifeless in comparison. However, it is precisely in this discomfort that the seeds of transformation are sown.

It is not uncommon for those unaccustomed to neutrality to experience a sense of disorientation and unease upon encountering this serene state. The absence of emotional peaks and valleys can leave us feeling adrift, as if we have been robbed of our sense of purpose and direction. Because we have been conditioned within a culture that glorifies achievement and ambition, the tranquility of neutrality can be mistaken for stagnation or indifference—feelings we may be programmed to reject. Yet, it is in this very discomfort that the true essence of growth resides.

Through The Process, we are invited to confront our discomfort head-on and to view the unsettling terrain of neutrality as a catalyst for personal evolution. Rather than shying away from the unfamiliar, we are encouraged to lean into the discomfort, trusting that it holds the key to our liberation. It is through this courageous act of surrender that we reclaim agency over our lives, transcending the confines of our conditioned patterns and beliefs.

Indeed, the journey towards neutrality requires determination and a willingness to confront the shadows lurking within, to sit with the discomfort of uncertainty, and to relinquish the false comforts of familiarity. Yet, it is only by traversing this tumultuous terrain that we can emerge on the other side, reborn in the light of our true essence.

Embracing neutrality demands a deep confrontation with our inner turmoil, urging us to reject our relentless pursuit of constant stimulation. In a world inundated with distractions, it calls upon us to cultivate a space of quiet introspection, where we can delve into the depths of our emotions without fear or avoidance. This journey requires a courageous willingness to sit with discomfort and work The Process to unravel its tangled threads and discern its underlying origins. Only by acknowledging and understanding our inner turmoil can we begin to escape its grasp and move towards a state of equanimity.

Central to achieving neutrality is the imperative to love ourselves unconditionally, embracing every facet of our being with tenderness and compassion. This self-love serves as the cornerstone upon which our temple of inner peace is built. By accepting and exploring all aspects of ourselves without judgment, we pave the way for healing and growth. Through this process, we come to recognize the inherent worthiness of our existence, finding solace in the knowledge that we are deserving of love and acceptance, both from ourselves and from others.

Ultimately, finding our motivation to embrace neutrality lies in understanding what truly matters to us at the core of our being. It entails a journey of self-discovery and introspection, wherein we unearth our deepest desires and aspirations. Armed with this newfound clarity, we can navigate life's complexities with a sense of purpose and direction. Embracing neutrality allows us to cultivate a life grounded in authenticity and integrity, where our actions are guided by love and compassion. It is a testament to our inherent capacity for growth and transformation, affirming our ability to live a life infused with meaning and fulfillment.

Navigating neutrality requires a delicate balance between patience and purpose. In the midst of this equilibrium, it is imperative to keep our gaze fixed on personal goals—those aspirations that illuminate the path towards a more fulfilled, confident, and loving self. However, the allure to fill the void of neutrality with any semblance of familiarity can be overpowering. This urge arises from the discomfort of encountering a state we're not accustomed to. Yet, the opportunity for growth and transformation lies within this discomfort.

In the void that can feel quite empty, it is important to hold that space until it is filled with positivity and light, because the universe can always deliver something better than what we can create ourselves. Embracing neutrality is not about rushing to fill the void, but rather about preserving the space it provides for introspection and alignment. By resisting the impulse to hastily occupy this emotional energetic void, we allow the universe the opportunity to orchestrate something greater, something that resonates with our elevated vibration. The universe communicates in the language of energy, and as we shed old patterns and beliefs that no longer serve us, we elevate our energetic frequency. This elevation paves the way for the universe to deliver manifestations that harmonize with our newfound resonance, thus ushering in a reality aligned with our highest intentions.

In navigating neutrality, it's crucial to trust in the inherent wisdom of the universe's unfolding. By patiently sitting with neutrality and remaining steadfast in our desire to live more authentically, we create a receptive space for the universe to deliver blessings that match our elevated vibration. This process is a testament to the transformative power of alignment and surrender, as we co-create our reality in harmony with the rhythms of the cosmos.

In the quest for enlightenment, embracing neutrality serves as a pivotal milestone along the spiritual journey. As a gateway to shedding the confines of the ego, it enables a profound connection with the fundamental truths that underpin existence. Within the realm of neutrality, one can experience the world through the lens of unconditional love, perceiving the inherent interconnectedness that binds all beings together in the tapestry of life. As we recognize the shared essence that unites every soul, we gain a profound sense of empathy and compassion. It becomes evident that our individual experiences are but facets of a larger, universal consciousness. Through this expansive perspective, we cultivate a deeper understanding of our interconnectedness with all of creation, fostering harmony and unity amidst the diversity of existence.

In this way neutrality empowers us to cultivate empathy and compassion towards ourselves and others. Instead of being driven by fear or desire, we can respond to life's challenges with grace and understanding. In doing so, we contribute to the collective evolution of consciousness, one moment of presence at a time.

However, it is important to acknowledge the path towards neutrality is not linear. You will encounter moments of resistance and setbacks along the way. Yet, each obstacle presents an opportunity for growth and self-dis-

Finding Neutrality

Kari, a seasoned therapist, had dedicated herself to cultivating resilience, navigating through her own trauma, and instilling the importance of setting boundaries in her clients' lives. With a profound understanding of boundaries, triggers, shadow work, and the language of self-love, she was deeply ingrained in the practice of advocating for healthy interpersonal dynamics. Her expertise made her a natural fit for exploring The Process. While working through The Process, she brought to light an aspect of The Process we had yet to thoroughly explore: the state of neutrality. This revelation proved to be eye-opening for Kari, as it unearthed the underlying motive behind her current relationship—a realization that she had unwittingly assumed the role of a savior for her partner, contrary to her years of counseling others to avoid such perilous patterns.

While dating someone who was in the midst of a divorce, Kari underwent a transformation as she confronted triggers linked to her partner's actions. It dawned on her that she was inadvertently assuming the role of a fixer in her partner's tumultuous divorce proceedings, driven by a subconscious desire to shield them from the emotional turmoil and legal complexities inherent in such circumstances. Reflecting on her own past experiences of navigating a comparable situation, Kari recognized a poignant pattern: she had subconsciously replicated a relationship dynamic to rescue her partner from the very heartaches and challenges she had endured when feeling abandoned and unsupported in her own past struggles.

Years earlier, Kari had traversed the challenging terrain of divorce herself, grappling with its emotional and logistical burdens without the aid of a supportive figure. Through the process of releasing triggers, she unveiled the deeper layers of her motivation in her current relationship, realizing she had unconsciously sought to provide the support and solace that had been absent in her own time of need. By using The Process, Kari was prompted to confront the parallels between her past and present, urging her to reassess her role in her partner's journey and to embark on a path of healing and empowerment that honored her own growth and resilience.

After using The Process to release the triggers she faced while in the relationship, Kari encountered a significant hurdle when she confronted the state of neutrality within herself. It prompted her to deeply question whether her primary driver in the relationship was rescuing her partner. As Kari relinquished the urge to be her partner's savior, she experienced a liberation from the emotional rollercoaster tied to her partner's predicament. This newfound detachment led her to confront the unsettling realization that what she had perceived as love might indeed be rooted in a savior complex.

With feelings of loss and emptiness, Kari, an educated therapist, found herself wrestling with the concept of neutrality, so do not be surprised if the concept also takes you by surprise. Working through those feelings is part of the courageous journey towards enlightenment, and this is when you learn to stay focused on your goals.

covery. By accepting the discomfort and returning to your true motivators, you can reaffirm your commitment to the path of enlightenment.

On this path towards personal growth and enlightenment, there often comes a point where we must confront discomfort head-on. In these moments of discomfort, the universe presents us with an opportunity for transformation. Instead of instinctively filling this discomfort with distractions or drama, we must learn to sit with it, allowing the universe to work its magic. By experiencing this discomfort, we open ourselves up to the possibility of profound change and growth. It is a process of surrendering to the unknown and trusting in the universe's wisdom.

When we resist sitting with discomfort and instead seek to fill the void with familiar distractions or emotional turmoil, we inadvertently limit our potential for growth. In doing so, we cling to old patterns and habits, preventing the universe from guiding us towards our true potential. By embracing neutrality and allowing ourselves to sit with the discomfort, we create space for the universe to align us with a new vibration—one that is more aligned with our goals of enlightenment, love, and compassion.

Embracing discomfort does not mean becoming complacent with our lives; rather, it is about staying focused on our goals while allowing the universe to orchestrate the necessary changes. We must continue to row our own boat, actively working towards our aspirations. However, by neutrally acknowledging our discomfort and remaining open to the universe's guidance, we pave the way for a deeper understanding of ourselves and a more meaningful journey towards becoming the enlightened, loving, and compassionate individuals we aspire to be.

Each time we navigate through The Process as we take more steps towards greater enlightenment, we will be called to choose the discomfort of neutrality and return to our true motivators. The ultimate goal of The Process is to reach a state of neutrality, which grants us the ability to observe events without being swept away by their emotional currents. Peace, calm, and neutrality may seem elusive in a society addicted to instant gratification and constant highs. However, by confronting our inner turmoil and reconnecting with our core values, we can transcend the chaos of our minds and emotions, allowing us to perceive the world with clarity and compassion. Neutrality is not an endpoint but rather a continuous journey towards enlightenment, fueled by the unwavering commitment to growth and self-awareness. Give yourself grace on this path because becoming comfortable with neutrality is not always an easy feat, especially in today's fast-paced society.

Embracing neutrality requires us to confront our inner turmoil and relinquish the relentless pursuit of constant stimulation. It calls upon us to cultivate a space of quiet introspection, where we can delve into the depths of our emotions without fear or avoidance. We must have the courage to willingly sit quietly with discomfort and work The Process to unravel its tangled threads and discern its underlying origins. Only by acknowledging and understanding our inner turmoil can we begin to transcend its grasp and move towards a state of equanimity. You are worth taking this courageous path and exploring neutrality.

Ultimately, finding your motivation to seek neutrality lies in under-standing what truly matters to you at the core of your being. Your deepest desires and aspirations will be unearthed as you incorporate The Process into your life, awakening your path of self-discovery and introspection. Embracing neutrality through The Process allows you to cultivate a life grounded in authenticity and integrity, where your actions are guided by love and compassion. Armed with this newfound clarity, you can navigate life's complexities with a sense of purpose and direction. Instead of being driven by fear or desire, you can respond to life's challenges with grace and understanding. Your inherent capacity for growth and transformation leads to a life infused with meaning and fulfillment that goes beyond the limitations of your ego. From a state of neutrality, you can view the world through the lens of unconditional love, recognizing the interconnectedness of all beings. In doing so, you contribute to the collective evolution of consciousness, one moment of presence at a time.

Remember, if you begin to feel lost while navigating through The Process, embrace the discomfort of neutrality and return to your true motivators. By confronting your inner turmoil and reconnecting with your core values, you can transcend the chaos and find true fulfillment.

All the courageous who decide to take this path know it may be fraught with challenges and discomfort; however, it is ultimately through relishing this unsettling journey that we pave the way for our own enlightenment. By transcending the lure of instant gratification and returning to our true motivators, we reclaim agency over our lives and embark on a journey of profound transformation. In the stillness of neutrality we find our truest selves, poised on the precipice of infinite possibility.

The process of self-discovery unravels the layers that shroud our true motivations and reveal the path towards becoming a more enlightened version of ourselves. By delving deep into the core of our being and stripping away the masks we wear, we unveil the innate beauty of our authentic selves—a perfect embodiment of unconditional love. At its essence, this journey is a testament to the profound practice of self-love, self-compassion, and self-forgiveness. Through introspection and reflection, we come to recognize that our capacity to give love and compassion to others is intrinsically linked to the love and compassion we cultivate within ourselves.

Each step in this journey of self-discovery is a confirmation of the transformative power of introspection and self-awareness. As we peel back the layers of conditioning and societal expectations, we uncover the raw authenticity of our true essence—a radiant being of love and light. This process isn't merely about uncovering superficial traits or accomplishments; it is about embracing the entirety of who we are, flaws and all, with a sense of reverence and acceptance. By acknowledging our imperfections and our vulnerabilities, we cultivate a deeper sense of self-compassion and understanding, paving the way for profound personal growth and transformation.

This journey of self-discovery is intrinsically intertwined with the notion of interconnectedness—the understanding that our inner state profoundly influences the world around us. As we travel this path of self-love and self-compassion, we come to recognize that the love and compassion we extend to ourselves naturally radiates outward, shaping our interactions and relationships with others. In essence, by nurturing the wellspring of love and compassion within ourselves, we empower ourselves to give generously to those around us, fostering a ripple effect of healing and transformation in our communities and beyond. Thus, the journey of self-discovery transcends individual growth; it's a profound testament to the interconnectedness of all beings and the transformative power of love.

We invite you to join us on this beautiful, messy journey of becoming our authentic selves!

Chapter 9

The Process

1. *The Process can be used when you are sitting quietly and not currently being triggered or when you are in the middle of a current situation where you are feeling triggered.*

   a. *If you are not triggered now, can you think of a time in the recent past when you were triggered? What are/were you feeling? What is/was coming up?*

   b. *If you are currently being triggered: What are/were you feeling? What is/was coming up?*

   To answer, describe an emotion such as annoyed, anger, helpless.

2. *Where do you feel that in your body?*

   There is no wrong answer. Could be solar plexus, crown, shoulders, etc.

3. *What name would you put on that feeling?*

   If you are having a hard time putting a name on the feeling, how do you sense it? What do you see (color, shape), hear, feel (temperature, soft, hard, fuzzy), taste, smell?

4. *Think back to the very first time you felt that exact emotion.*

   Remember emotions have different modalities. For example, anger, shame, fear all have different micro feelings within them that make up the overall larger emotion. Home in on the micro feelings of the larger emotion.

5. *When was the first time you remember feeling that exact emotion?*

   Past life ,invitro, after birth (PL/I/AB)?

   Your answer to this question can be affected by your belief system and that is okay! If you do not believe in past or parallel lives, then you will not choose that as an answer. Again, that is fine. Take the first feeling you sense and do not judge or criticize that feeling.

6. *Could you feel into yourself at that moment? What did you need that you did not get?*

7. *Can you surround that part of yourself and offer yourself what you needed in that moment? If not, can you identify someone, alive or passed, who can?*

   Did you need compassion and understanding? Did you need someone to step in and protect you? Sometimes we need to completely reimagine the scene with a different outcome.

8. *Now go back to the situation you are investigating that triggered you today (or recently). What are you feeling now?*

   The goal is to arrive at a place of neutrality where you can observe a situation happening and choose a response from a place of energetic neutrality. If you still feel triggering energy around the situation, run through the process again. Sometimes, when we think back to the first time we had that exact emotion (#4), we do not go far enough back.

9. *Bring that feeling of neutrality to the trigger. Can you notice that you can make a different choice?*

10. It is important to know you took yourself as far as you could today.

Love yourself as you are and celebrate the work you did today. Sometimes we are not ready to fully release a trigger and will have to revisit it. That is okay! You made progress just addressing the situation. Honor that progress.

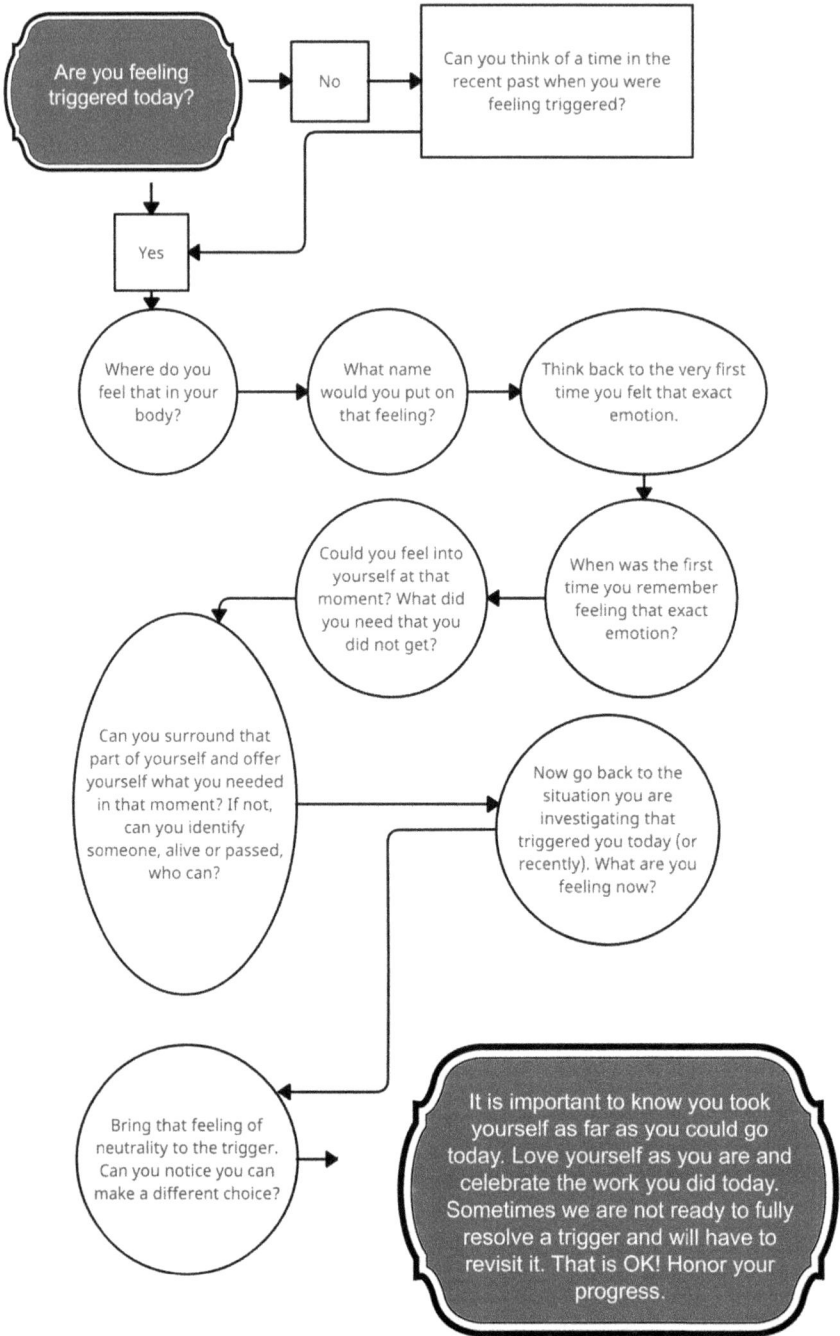

Are you feeling triggered today?

No → Can you think of a time in the recent past when you were feeling triggered?

Yes

Where do you feel that in your body?

What name would you put on that feeling?

Think back to the very first time you felt that exact emotion.

When was the first time you remember feeling that exact emotion?

Could you feel into yourself at that moment? What did you need that you did not get?

Can you surround that part of yourself and offer yourself what you needed in that moment? If not, can you identify someone, alive or passed, who can?

Now go back to the situation you are investigating that triggered you today (or recently). What are you feeling now?

Bring that feeling of neutrality to the trigger. Can you notice you can make a different choice?

It is important to know you took yourself as far as you could go today. Love yourself as you are and celebrate the work you did today. Sometimes we are not ready to fully resolve a trigger and will have to revisit it. That is OK! Honor your progress.

Diving Deep

Case Studies

We have been blessed with the incredible opportunity to work with hundreds of people over the years, walking alongside them as they embarked on their spiritual journeys and personal transformations. Together, we have lovingly developed The Process, a system designed to guide people towards deeper self-awareness, healing, and growth. Every person who has come to us, whether through one-on-one sessions or group workshops, has enriched our lives, as we've witnessed the unfolding of incredible moments of transformation, clarity, and purpose.

From the very beginning, we dedicated ourselves to ensuring The Process remained accessible and as straightforward as possible—because we know that spiritual awakening doesn't have to be complicated to be powerful. In fact, we believe the most profound shifts often happen in the simplest moments of deep connection, self-reflection, and inner clarity. While we have carefully honed this system over time, our hearts have always stayed focused on making it a safe, supportive, and nurturing space for each person to step into.

Spiritual awakening and personal growth are deeply intimate and individualized experiences. No two paths are ever the same, and we approach every session and every workshop with this in mind. Our first priority is always to truly listen—not just to the words our clients speak but also to the unspoken emotions and energies that each person carries with them. We know how important it is for people to feel seen and heard, to feel that their journey is being honored with compassion and respect. And it is in this sacred space of listening that we are able to offer the most meaningful guidance, helping each person connect to their own inner wisdom and truth.

Through our work, we have witnessed countless people grow in confidence, find healing from past wounds, and step more fully into their authentic selves. We've watched families come together in harmony, with old tensions dissolving into newfound understanding. We've seen groups of people expand their spiritual awareness, supporting one another as they explore the deeper layers of their consciousness. These are the moments that reaffirm The Process works, not just as a tool for personal development, but as a way of cultivating love, healing, and community.

As we look back on the incredible journey of developing The Process and publishing Awakening Your Path, we feel immense gratitude for every person who has trusted us with their spiritual growth. The stories shared on the following pages are a reflection of those journeys—of the courage, authenticity, and grace each person has brought to our work. Out of respect for their privacy, we have changed the names in these case studies.

Being a part of someone's spiritual awakening is not just a profession for us—it is a privilege we hold close to our hearts. We are continually inspired by the strength, vulnerability, and beauty of the people we work with. Every person's path is as unique as they are, and we remain dedicated to walking alongside each person with the same loving care and compassion that has always been at the core of our work.

Releasing Anxiety

This case study demonstrates how The Process was used to help Kevin, who grappled with chronic anxiety. Interestingly, Kevin didn't perceive his anxiety as an obstacle; rather, he viewed it as a driving force pushing him towards greater achievements. However, despite his acceptance of this condition, he realized it adversely impacted his interpersonal relationships and well-being, preventing him from experiencing moments of tranquility and calm.

1. *Can you think of a time in the recent past when you were triggered?*

   The trigger occurred as Kevin engaged in a group project. Instead of embracing the collective flow of ideas and team synergy, he felt driven to intervene, imposing his pace on others. It is important to note that this was not an instance where creativity and workflow had stalled. Kevin just felt the need to account for and control all outcomes and the flow of the meeting. His frenzied energy disrupted the creative atmosphere and hindered meaningful progress.

2. *Where do you feel that in your body?*

   There is no wrong answer. Could be solar plexus, crown, shoulders, etc.

   Kevin felt the emotion in his solar plexus area, but it radiated from his solar plexus into his entire body.

3. *What name would you put on that feeling?*

Kevin identified the emotion as anxiety brought on by the need to account for all outcomes in all situations.

4. *Think back to the very first time you felt that exact emotion.*

The primary emotion—anxiety—brought on the need to control all aspects of his life because he felt that in control there is safety.

5. *When was the first time you remember feeling that exact emotion?*

Past life ,invitro, after birth (PL/I/AB)?

It is crucial to trust the initial response that arises when posed with a question and refrain from passing judgment. Kevin's immediate response was that he was invitro. His mother's high level of anxiety deeply influenced Kevin, leading him to absorb that anxiety himself. Although Kevin's exposure to his mother's anxiety throughout his upbringing further entrenched this behavior, to truly address the trigger, it was essential for him to trace back to the earliest instance of experiencing that specific emotion.

6. *Could you feel into yourself at that moment? What did you need that you did not get?*

Kevin expressed he needed a peaceful and calm environment to be able to thrive as he grew, not only in the womb, but as a child.

7. *Can you surround that part of yourself and offer yourself what you needed in that moment? If not, can you identify someone, alive or passed, who can?*

Did you need compassion and understanding? Did you need someone to step in and protect you?

Because of the relationship Kevin had with his mother and his mother's inability to take responsibility for her actions, Kevin could not envision his mother surrounding him with peace, calm, and love. Instead, Kevin brought in an Aunt to surround him with those feelings. He envisioned himself invitro and his Aunt coming in to fully encapsulate him in the feelings of love, calm, peace, and compassion. By focusing on his Aunt's presence and the positive emotions associated with it, Kevin essentially created a safe haven within himself, a place where he can find solace and thrive despite the challenges presented by his relationship with his mother. This ability to cultivate inner peace and resilience is truly admirable.

8. *Now go back to the original triggering situation. Now what are you feeling?*

   The goal is to arrive at a place of neutrality where you can observe a situation happening and choose a response from a place of energetic neutrality. If you still feel triggering energy around the situation, run through the process again. Sometimes, when we think back to the first time we had that exact emotion (#4), we do not go far enough back.

   Kevin was able to see himself within the group project as an observer, enabling him to fully witness and appreciate everyone's contributions. He experienced himself as an onlooker in the midst of a splendid collaborative endeavor.

9. *Bring that feeling of neutrality to the trigger. Can you notice you can make a different choice?*

   Kevin's experience with The Process had a transformative effect on him. He felt an immediate release of anxiety and could relinquish the need to not only push himself but those around him. He not only was able to make a different choice in that moment, but he immediately realized how the anxiety had affected all aspects of his life. Not everyone is able to immediately link the trigger released in the scenario they are working on to other aspects of their life.

   The fact that Kevin no longer felt the need to push himself or control those around him indicated a shift in his mindset towards a more balanced and collaborative approach. His frenetic energy immediately dissipated, and it even surprised him how he was no longer feeling the need to control the team he was working with.

Later, Kevin did express he felt a little lost without the ever-present anxiety that had driven him for his entire lifetime. Releasing feelings that have been with us our entire lives, whether it be anger, drama, anxiety, or unworthiness, can leave us grappling with the question of what to fill that void with. Of course, love is the answer. We can feel detached from life as we are unaccustomed to the feeling of neutrality. However, neutrality doesn't mean indifference or detachment; rather, it involves observing thoughts and emotions without judgment or attachment. By cultivating neutrality, we can navigate the ups and downs of life with greater ease and clarity, without being driven solely by past habits or emotions.

10. *It is important to know you took yourself as far as you could today.*

Love yourself as you are and celebrate the work you did today. Sometimes we are not ready to fully release a trigger and will have to revisit it. That is okay! You made progress just addressing the situation. Honor that progress.

The Process: Case Study 2

Releasing the Need for Drama

This case study illustrates the application of The Process in a situation involving Candice, who consistently finds herself surrounded by drama, despite claiming to dislike it and being unaware of her role in creating it. Candace remained oblivious to how her daily decisions contributed to the drama, yet anyone familiar with her would readily highlight her tendency to stir up drama, both personally and professionally.

1. *Can you think of a time in the recent past when you were triggered?*

   In this instance, Candace was instructed to go back to the most recent time drama had come her way.

2. *Where do you feel that in your body?*

   There is no wrong answer. Could be solar plexus, crown, shoulders, etc.

   Candace was able to identify where in her body she felt the heightened sense of emotion, which was in her chest. Drama can feel differently to each person, and each person can feel it in a different area.

3. *What name would you put on that feeling?*

   The emotion attached to the dramatic event was anger.

4. *Think back to the very first time you felt that exact emotion.*

The primary emotion she felt was anger, accompanied by a secondary feeling of sadness. It is understandable if you cannot pinpoint the precise name for the secondary emotion; what matters most is experiencing and acknowledging it fully.

5. *When was the first time you remember feeling that exact emotion?*

Past life ,invitro, after birth (PL/I/AB)?

Candace was able to first identify after birth and then that she was verbal. She was a little girl of about five. She recalled a memory of her family interacting and when she felt completely ignored, unheard, and unseen.

6. *Could you feel into yourself at that moment? What did you need that you did not get?*

When she felt into herself as that little girl, she needed attention and to feel she mattered. Candace had spent most of her life feeling as if she did not "fit" into her family and as if she was an observer of her family's activities instead of a participant in them.

7. *Can you surround that part of yourself and offer yourself what you needed in that moment? If not, can you identify someone, alive or passed, who can?*

Did you need compassion and understanding? Did you need someone to step in and protect you? Sometimes we need to completely reimagine the scene with a different outcome.

In this instance, Candace imagined her mother turning and stooping down to her level, looking her in the eye with her full attention and asking Candace for her opinion. Her mother then told Candace how important her opinion was and how important her presence was at their family event and then enveloped her in a hug.

8. *Now go back to the original triggering situation. Now what are you feeling?*

   The goal is to arrive at a place of neutrality where you can observe a situation happening and choose a response from a place of energetic neutrality. If you still feel triggering energy around the situation, run through the process again. Sometimes, when we think back to the first time we had that exact emotion (#4), we do not go far enough back.

   Candace had long been entrenched in a cycle of attracting drama throughout her life. The behaviors that fuel this drama had become so deeply ingrained that they permeated every aspect of her existence, functioning almost as reflexively as breathing. While Candace managed to revisit a recent work-related situation and release the associated energy, acknowledging her role in generating much of the drama in her life proved to be challenging. Consequently, she struggled to let go of the triggers linked to her personal life. When our self-perception is challenged—Candace has always been perplexed by the abundance of drama, as she adamantly dislikes it—it can be a gradual process to accept and internalize new insights. At this juncture, it's vital to extend ourselves compassion and support, speaking to ourselves with the kindness and understanding we would offer to a dear friend, recognizing the progress we've made thus far.

9. *Bring that feeling of neutrality to the trigger. Can you notice you can make a different choice?*

   Candace not only identified how she could have made a different choice in that moment but also carried that insight into future work relationships. Consequently, her work performance has undergone a complete transformation, leading to a more amicable relationship with her colleagues and significant monetary gains.

10. *It is important to know you took yourself as far as you could today.*

   Love yourself as you are and celebrate the work you did today. Sometimes we are not ready to fully release a trigger and will have to revisit it. That is okay! You made progress just addressing the situation. Honor that progress.

Accepting Assistance

This case study demonstrates how The Process was helpful to Kaitlynn, who received a cancer diagnosis. Coping with a severe illness typically involves many complex layers. We collaborated closely with Kaitlynn over several months to address her triggers. Some triggers bore similarities, and as one layer was addressed, deeper layers emerged. Throughout her transformative journey, numerous triggers surfaced, reflecting the intricate nature of her situation.

1. *Can you think of a time in the recent past when you were triggered?*

   She recognized her trigger as her friends and family stepped forward to offer assistance, whether through financial support or by running errands and similar tasks.

2. *Where do you feel that in your body?*

   There is no wrong answer. Could be solar plexus, crown, shoulders, etc.

   Kaitlynn felt the emotion in her solar plexus area.

3. *What name would you put on that feeling?*

   Kaitlynn identified the emotion as anxiety brought on by fear.

4. *Think back to the very first time you felt that exact emotion.*

With the primary emotion being anxiety brought on by fear, Kaitlynn was able to identify the first time she could remember that emotion.

5. *When was the first time you remember feeling that exact emotion?*

Past life ,invitro, after birth (PL/I/AB)?

Kaitlynn was able to first identify after birth and then that she was verbal. At the age of five, she fell ill with a cough that progressed into the flu and a severe cough. The severity of the cough frightened her, although she later realized as an adult that she had been ill with croup. One night, she woke up coughing, disturbing her mother who became increasingly agitated, loudly expressing her displeasure about the disturbance in the house. As Kaitlynn's illness persisted, her mother threatened to take her to the hospital, a prospect that terrified her. In her threat to take Kaitlynn to the hospital, her mother portrayed hospitals as frightening places where ominous events occurred, not as locations for healing. Kaitlynn vividly remembered burying her face in a pillow to muffle her cough, fearing the consequences of being taken to the hospital and left there.

6. *Could you feel into yourself at that moment? What did you need that you did not get?*

Kaitlynn expressed the necessity for understanding and compassion. She also desired solitude to endure sickness without the disturbance of constant admonishments or threats of unsettling situations.

7. *Can you surround that part of yourself and offer yourself what you needed in that moment? If not, can you identify someone, alive or passed, who can?*

Did you need compassion and understanding? Did you need someone to step in and protect you?

Kaitlynn imagined herself in a beautiful room with a soft comfortable bed and with a loving mother who came and checked on her every so often with compassion.

8. *Now go back to the original triggering situation. Now what are you feeling?*

   The goal is to arrive at a place of neutrality where you can observe a situation happening and choose a response from a place of energetic neutrality. If you still feel triggering energy around the situation, run through the process again. Sometimes, when we think back to the first time we had that exact emotion (#4), we do not go far enough back.

   During her initial encounter, Kaitlynn managed to release the trigger, allowing herself to perceive the situation with neutrality. However, as more offers of assistance poured in, she found herself being triggered again, though to a lesser degree. Some instances of support exceeded her expectations, thrusting her into the limelight. This spotlight, though challenging for most, proved even more difficult for Kaitlynn given its association with her illness, which had conditioned her to view assistance in a negative light. She worked through The Process three times before she felt comfortable accepting help.

9. *Bring that feeling of neutrality to the trigger. Can you notice you can make a different choice?*

   Kaitlynn became comfortable with accepting help graciously and in harmony with the loving vibration with which it was given.

10. *It is important to know you took yourself as far as you could today.*

   Love yourself as you are and celebrate the work you did today. Sometimes we are not ready to fully release a trigger and will have to revisit it. That is okay! You made progress just addressing the situation. Honor that progress.

Pinpointing Your Triggers

This case study demonstrates how to determine where your triggers are. Some of us have become so adept at tamping down our emotions and distancing ourselves from situations that cause us angst, we do not recognize them as a trigger.

1. *Can you think of a time in the recent past when you were triggered?*

   Initially, when questioned, Carol asserted that she never experiences triggering events. We then asked if she could recall a recent time when she changed her behavior because of unease someone caused her. Carol described a recent incident where she consciously avoided encountering a resident of her apartment complex. Whenever Carol noticed this person heading towards a path intersecting with hers, she deliberately altered her route to evade any potential interaction.

2. *Where do you feel that in your body?*

   There is no wrong answer. Could be solar plexus, crown, shoulders, etc.

   Carol was asked about the physical sensations she experiences when she notices that specific person approaching her and decides to alter her course. She explained that initially, she feels a tightening in her stomach, followed swiftly by that feeling spreading to her chest and then upward into her head.

3. *What name would you put on that feeling?*

Carol grappled momentarily to identify the name of the emotion, a common challenge for those skilled at suppressing their feelings. (Had she failed to pinpoint an emotion after a brief pause, she would have been prompted to associate a color with the energy shift. Following this case study, a brief paragraph will explain the process to use if a person cannot name an emotion and they can only give the energy shift a color.)

4. *Think back to the very first time you felt that exact emotion.*

Carol was able to move her attention to her stomach where the emotion was the strongest and sit with the feeling of fear and separateness.

5. *When was the first time you remember feeling that exact emotion?*

Past life ,invitro, after birth (PL/I/AB)?

Carol was able to first identify after birth and then that she was verbal. She then recalled an incident where she saw herself as a young girl of about eight at a bible study held at her home church. Despite being unable to recall the events leading up to it, she vividly remembered another girl from the study group jumping on her, pushing her to the ground, and choking her. The image of the girl approaching and choking her remained clear in her memory.

6. *Could you feel into yourself at that moment? What did you need that you did not get?*

Carol needed protection and refuge. She perpetually sensed a disconnect, feeling like a magnet for bullies. She yearned for someone to intervene and shield her, reassuring her of her place and safety in any setting.

7. *Can you surround that part of yourself and offer yourself what you needed in that moment? If not, can you identify someone, alive or passed, who can?*

   Did you need compassion and understanding? Did you need someone to step in and protect you?

   Carol envisioned the responsible adult stepping in to protect her. With this image in mind, she could connect with her heart, embracing herself with unconditional love and a sense of belonging. Drawing from this feeling, she enveloped other sporadic memories that surfaced until she reached the present moment.

8. *Now go back to the original triggering situation. Now what are you feeling?*

   The goal is to arrive at a place of neutrality where you can observe a situation happening and choose a response from a place of energetic neutrality. If you still feel triggering energy around the situation, run through the process again. Sometimes, when we think back to the first time we had that exact emotion (#4), we do not go far enough back.

   When she envisioned the person walking down the hall, Carol was able to see herself confidently striding past her now.

9. *Bring that feeling of neutrality to the trigger. Can you notice you can make a different choice?*

   Carol reported back later that letting go of this mental barrier empowered her to confidently embrace other situations, including new adventures she had once shied away from due to the fear of not belonging or being judged. Carol also recognized the reason she had been triggered by the other person is because the other person has memory problems and can become easily agitated acting out aggressively, not physically, but loudly and belligerently with their words.

10. It is important to know you took yourself as far as you could today.

Love yourself as you are and celebrate the work you did today. Sometimes we are not ready to fully release a trigger and will have to revisit it. That is okay! You made progress just addressing the situation. Honor that progress.

Losing a Loved One

This case study demonstrates how the journey of grief can be hindered by triggers and how The Process can bring peace after losing someone close to you.

1. *Can you think of a time in the recent past when you were triggered?*

   Justin, also known as JJ, recently experienced the loss of someone he was casually seeing. Following a night out, they returned home and fell into bed in the early hours of the morning, utterly exhausted. Upon waking up a couple of hours later, JJ discovered that his partner had passed away. Despite administering CPR until first responders arrived, JJ's partner couldn't be revived. Since then, JJ has found himself trapped in grief, struggling to navigate the overwhelming emotions tied to this tragic event.

2. *Where do you feel that in your body?*

   There is no wrong answer. Could be solar plexus, crown, shoulders, etc.

   JJ sensed the emotion welling up in his chest and tightening in his throat, feeling as though he were choking on it.

3. *What name would you put on that feeling?*

   The sensation JJ experienced was one of loneliness. Despite having many friends and a strong support network, he was taken aback when he recognized the feeling of being isolated and unsupported. Furthermore, he felt as though no one truly comprehended the depth of what he was enduring.

4. *Think back to the very first time you felt that exact emotion.*

   JJ was instructed to sit with that exact feeling of loneliness where he felt as though no one truly comprehended the depth of his suffering.

5. *When was the first time you remember feeling that exact emotion?*

   Past life ,invitro, after birth (PL/I/AB)?

   While JJ had never previously pondered the concept of past lives, his initial instinct was that this experience resonated with a past life. Upon reflection, he was able to discern a previous existence where he had suffered the loss of both a child and, shortly before the loss of his child, his spouse had passed.

6. *Could you feel into yourself at that moment? What did you need that you did not get?*

   JJ expressed that the paramount need he felt was for support and a sense of belonging within a community. Reflecting on the past life, he recalled feeling isolated and ostracized, with people keeping their distance from him.

7. *Can you surround that part of yourself and offer yourself what you needed in that moment? If not, can you identify someone, alive or passed, who can?*

   Did you need compassion and understanding? Did you need someone to step in and protect you?

   JJ imagined people encircling him with compassion and empathy. Instead of attempting to remedy his grief and loss, they simply provided support and reassurance, letting him know that he was not alone in his struggles.

8. *Now go back to the original triggering situation. Now what are you feeling?*

   The goal is to arrive at a place of neutrality where you can observe a situation happening and choose a response from a place of energetic neutrality. If you still feel triggering energy around the situation, run through the process again. Sometimes, when we think back to the first time we had that exact emotion (#4), we do not go far enough back.

   When he visualized the loss in this current lifetime, he found himself less entrenched in grief. While he still experienced the weight of the loss, the feelings of guilt and the sense of being unable to progress in life had diminished. JJ reported feeling much lighter.

9. *Bring that feeling of neutrality to the trigger. Can you notice you can make a different choice?*

   Weeks later, JJ shared how those around him noticed a significant change in his demeanor, with many inquiring about what he had done, remarking on how much happier and lighter he appeared. This transformation was evident in the decisions he was making to cultivate a more stable and uncomplicated life, embracing each moment instead of being weighed down by grief.

10. *It is important to know you took yourself as far as you could today.*

   Love yourself as you are and celebrate the work you did today. Sometimes we are not ready to fully release a trigger and will have to revisit it. That is okay! You made progress just addressing the situation. Honor that progress.

The Process

Worksheet

The Process Worksheet

To download a printable PDF of The Process Worksheet,
turn to the last page of this book for a QR code.

1. *The Process can be used when you are sitting quietly and not currently being triggered or when you are in the middle of a current situation where you are feeling triggered.*

   a. If you are not triggered now, can you think of a time in the recent past when you were triggered? What are/were you feeling? What is/was coming up?

   b. If you are currently being triggered: What are/were you feeling? What is/was coming up?

   To answer, describe an emotion such as annoyed, anger, helpless.

2. *Where do you feel that in your body?*

   There is no wrong answer. Could be solar plexus, crown, shoulders, etc.

3. *What name would you put on that feeling?*

    If you are having a hard time putting a name on the feeling, how do you sense it? What do you see (color, shape), hear, feel (temperature, soft, hard, fuzzy), taste, smell?

4. *Think back to the very first time you felt that exact emotion.*

    Remember emotions have different modalities. For example, anger, shame, fear all have different micro feelings within them that make up the overall larger emotion. Home in on the micro feelings of the larger emotion.

5. When was the first time you remember feeling that exact
    emotion?

    Past life ,invitro, after birth (PL/I/AB)?

    Your answer to this question can be affected by your belief
    system and that is okay! If you do not believe in past or
    parallel lives, then you will not choose that as an answer.
    Again, that is fine. Take the first feeling you sense and do
    not judge or criticize that feeling.

6. Could you feel into yourself at that moment? What did you
    need that you did not get?

7. *Can you surround that part of yourself and offer yourself what you needed in that moment? If not, can you identify someone, alive or passed, who can?*

   Did you need compassion and understanding? Did you need someone to step in and protect you? Sometimes we need to completely reimagine the scene with a different outcome.

8. *Now go back to the situation you are investigating that triggered you today (or recently). What are you feeling now?*

   The goal is to arrive at a place of neutrality where you can observe a situation happening and choose a response from a place of energetic neutrality. If you still feel triggering energy around the situation, run through the process again. Sometimes, when we think back to the first time we had that exact emotion (#4), we do not go far enough back.

9. *Bring that feeling of neutrality to the trigger. Can you notice that you can make a different choice?*

10. *It is important to know you took yourself as far as you could today.*

    Love yourself as you are and celebrate the work you did today. Sometimes we are not ready to fully release a trigger and will have to revisit it. That is okay! You made progress just addressing the situation. Honor that progress.

Epilogue

Amidst the cacophony of self-help offerings, Awaking Your Path emerges as a beacon of clarity, illuminating your path towards inner peace and liberation. Within these pages lies a tested methodology, The Process, designed to dismantle the triggers that tether you to suffering.

Picture this: you stand on the threshold of self-discovery, armed with the potent tool of inquiry—The Process. With each question posed, you delve deeper into the recesses of your psyche, unraveling the tangled web of triggers that shape your emotional landscape. From the mundane to the profound, no trigger remains untouched as you confront the root cause of your discontent.

Along your voyage, you encounter fellow travelers, each navigating their own labyrinth of triggers with courage and resilience. Their stories, woven into the fabric of this life's journey, serve as beacons of hope and inspiration, reminding you that transformation is not only possible but inevitable. Envision, if you will, standing at the crossroads of your emotional terrain, where every trigger, every impulse, loses its power to sway you. This is the essence of neutrality—a haven of tranquility amidst life's tempestuous currents. This revelation is akin to stumbling upon buried treasure, a guiding light illuminating your path towards newfound freedom and clarity.

Yet, here's the revelation: awakening isn't solely about discovering peace amidst chaos; it's about embracing chaos as an inherent facet of the human journey. It's about acknowledging that the path to self-discovery is intricate and nonlinear, fraught with twists and turns that defy rationality. And on your path, The Process stands as your steadfast companion, navigating you through the darkest recesses of your mind with unwavering patience and compassion.

As you turn the final page of Awakening Your Path, you're not bidding farewell to a book but rather embarking on a new chapter of your personal evolution. Here, amidst the echoes of newfound clarity and inner peace, you realize that awakening is not a destination but a continuous journey—one marked by growth, discovery, and profound self-awareness.

So, dear reader, as you reach the final chapter of Awakening Your Path, know that the journey doesn't end here. It's just the beginning of a new chapter in your life, one filled with endless possibilities and untapped potential. And if you're hungry for more wisdom, more guidance, and more stories of triumph over adversity, we invite you to join us on this journey through our courses, our books, our community, and our shared pursuit of awakening. Together, let us navigate the labyrinth of triggers, armed with nothing but the unwavering belief in our own capacity to transform.

About the Authors

Christy Godwin

Christy is a compassionate psychic, medium, healer, and life coach dedicated to guiding clients toward healing, growth, and fulfillment. With her unique blend of spiritual insight, empathy, and intuitive abilities, Christy has committed her life to helping others overcome obstacles, heal from traumas, and discover their true purpose.

From a young age, Christy recognized her intuitive gifts and deep connection with the spiritual realm. She has spent years honing these abilities, dedicating herself to serving others. Her journey into spirituality and holistic healing began with a profound awakening that led her to embrace her true calling.

As a psychic medium, Christy connects clients with departed loved ones, providing messages, guidance, and closure. In her healing practice, she addresses energetic blockages to support deep restoration and balance. As a life coach, she empowers clients to release triggers, remove barriers to their personal growth, and unlock their inner strength.

Christy's ultimate goal is to help clients find inner peace, embrace authenticity, and realize their dreams. With a Bachelor's degree in Child Development and a Master's degree in Business with a concentration in Finance, she has over 30 years of teaching experience, including more than 20 years at the collegiate level. Her mission is to spread love, healing, and positivity, fostering a community where inner peace and authentic living are accessible to everyone.

Christy holds numerous certifications, including Certified Life Coach, Akashic Records Practitioner, Advanced Soul Plan Reader, Psychic Investigator, Spiritual Advisor, Reiki Master, and Hypnotherapist. Through her gifts and dedication, Christy serves as a beacon of light, love, and hope, making a positive impact on many lives by helping them navigate challenges with grace and resilience.

Her work is a testament to the power of the human spirit and the profound impact one person can have on the lives of others. Christy cherishes the privilege of guiding souls toward their aspirations and fostering their growth into their best selves.

Iris Libby

Iris is an empathetic astrologer, psychic medium, and trance channeler with over 35 years of experience dedicated to guiding clients towards personal transformation and spiritual alignment. Applying her skills of astrological insight, intuition, and practical wisdom, Iris has committed her life to helping others connect with their cosmic blueprint, navigate life's challenges, and unlock their full potential.

Iris's spiritual quest began with a transformative astrology reading in New York City, which sparked her deep fascination with the stars and their guidance. Over the years, she has honed her ability to interpret the energies, potentials, and influences shaping clients' lives, offering them clarity and direction.

Iris's career path has been anything but conventional. Alongside her spiritual journey, she excelled in the corporate world, leveraging her intuitive gifts to lead and innovate in high-pressure environments. As Acting Director of Talent Acquisition at Amazon, she worked with management to build pipelines of candidates as well as fill key senior leadership roles. Prior to her time at Amazon, she was Chief Operating Officer and Managing Partner of Corcoran Group Marketing, Inc., and Senior Vice President of the Corcoran Group, Inc. Her corporate background has uniquely equipped her to blend practical business insights with spiritual guidance, making her advice both grounded and visionary.

Building on her corporate success, Iris always remained connected to her spiritual side, using astrology and intuition to guide her professional decisions. This balance of corporate leadership and spiritual insight has shaped Iris into a practical yet deeply insightful guide for others. As a Certified Spiritual Advisor, she integrates her business acumen with her intuitive abilities to help clients tap into their own inner guidance, navigating both their personal and professional lives with clarity and purpose.

Ultimately Iris's objective is to help others find clarity, inner peace, and alignment with their highest potential. She believes that by listening to the universe's wisdom and trusting our inner voices, we can live lives of greater purpose and fulfillment. Her work is a testament to her own journey—one that has balanced corporate leadership with deep spiritual exploration—and she cherishes the opportunity to help guide you in awakening your path.

Your Journey Continues...

Thank You for Walking This Path With Us

Christy and Iris are honored to have shared this journey with you. Your healing and awakening matter.

Scan the QR code to explore opportunities to work more closely with Christy and Iris and to receive free downloads of The Process worksheets to support your continued growth and transformation.

Your path is just beginning—let's keep walking it together.

With much love and light,

Christy & Iris

www.ingramcontent.com/pod-product-compliance
Lightning Source LLC
Chambersburg PA
CBHW051830090426
42736CB00011B/1737